God

IS SO

God!

The Adventures of a Traveling Ministry

on a Prophetic Faith Journey

Brenda Peters

Foreword by Ben R. Peters

God Is So God!
Copyright © 2004 by Brenda Joyce Peters

ISBN 0-9767685-3-4

Unless otherwise indicated, Bible quotations are taken from the New King James Version. Copyright © 1983 by Thomas Nelson, Inc.

Cover art by Jennifer Bartow Waters
www.bartowimages.com

Open Heart Ministries
15648 Bombay Blvd.
S. Beloit, IL 61080
www.ohmint.org
benrpeters@juno.com

Contents

Foreword

A s the husband of Brenda Peters, I have had the privilege
of sharing most of the experiences recorded in this
book. My life has been greatly enriched by living with such a
dynamic, compassionate and energetic, and yet very human,
woman of God. Most of the actual writing was done by me
with input from her, but the stories are pretty much as she
has told them in hundreds of locations, both in North
America and in other nations of the world.

God has given Brenda an unusual addiction to minister
to people in any kind of need. I have seen her give of her
time and energy in an incredibly sacrificial way. She has a
powerful compassion for hurting people of all ages. I have
tried to get her to back off at times from ministering to so
many people when she is already exhausted. She tells me
that when the Holy Spirit focuses her on someone, it's like
she cannot do anything else but go to them and completely

release the word that comes to her. She can't think of her own physical exhaustion or headache or backache, as long as the anointing is there to minister.

I am very confident that you will be challenged and motivated to walk with God and to deepen your relationship with Him as you read the stories recorded in this small book. It is our prayer that you will identify with many of our experiences and receive courage and strength to run your own race and finish your course.

God will use all who are willing to pay the price of dying to their own ambitions to seek first the Kingdom of God and His righteousness. That includes you. Please receive the Love of God into your own heart and life as you read the stories in this book. And should you desire to communicate with us for any reason, please feel free to use the information on the back of the book.

If you have never begun your own adventure with God and have not invited Jesus into your life as Lord and Savior, He is waiting for you to talk to Him and invite Him to lead you into your destiny. It simply involves confessing your sin and receiving His forgiveness, and then inviting Him to be your Savior and Lord.

Enjoy!!!

Ben R. Peters
President and Co-founder, Open Heart Ministries, Int.

CHAPTER 1

The Faith Journey Begins

Fulfilling My Own Prophecy

It was my own fault – this terrible time of transition trauma. Yes, I was the one that had prophesied in a room full of leaders that we were going to sell everything, get an RV and travel full-time. Was I crazy? I don't even like to camp! What had I gotten myself into? We were giving up a spacious house in North Spokane and preparing to live full time in a 33 foot trailer. The trailer would be pulled with a Chevy van. Our only plan was to go and minister wherever God sent us. Nobody had to tell me that we were crazy; that was all too obvious.

But we were doing it. And what a challenge! Frequent garage sales, trips to the storage unit and the garbage dump kept us busy for several weeks before we could load up a few precious items into the trailer that had been given to us by some good folk in Illinois. The large house we had been renting also had a large garage, packed full of stuff, most of which we had accumulated over thirty years of marriage. We were also storing things for our two daughters, Barbie and Andrea, who didn't have anywhere else to store them. It was a mind-boggling task.

The stress was almost more than I could handle. I had the job of making most of the tough decisions of what to sell, what to give away, what to throw away, what to store in one single garage size storage unit, and what to take with us on our journey. It was one of the most traumatic times in my adult life. It was a time of saying good-bye to some long-time treasures. Even the things that sold in the garage sales were practically given away. Coffee tables, made by a carpenter friend twenty years before, got us just a few dollars each.

Other little treasures like stuffed animals were also practically given away. Actually, a lot of things were given away. The only good thing about it was that I had a lot of things to give to the children I encountered in church or wherever. The money that did come from the garage sales came in very handy, because our income had almost dried up from all other sources.

Taking Our Boys Through Transition Trauma

Besides my own emotional stress, I had to find ways to encourage our two boys, Timothy, age 11, and Nathan, age 9. They loved their Christian School, which was run by their big brother, Ken, along with his lovely wife, Valencia. Ken and Valencia had such a great gift for making school fun and exciting. In addition, the boys had some good friends that they did not want to leave behind in Spokane. They would also have to leave behind their new bikes and most of their toys and games, because there just wasn't enough room in the trailer for most of their stuff. They had to make decisions just like I did. Some things went in garage sales. Other things went to storage. Only a few choice items were allowed in the trailer. Nathan, the younger, had the hardest time saying good-bye to his precious possessions. So my tears were flowing for them as well as for myself, while, at the same time I had to be strong to encourage them.

My husband, Ben, tried to be understanding and kept on working with me to get us ready to move out by September 1, but my emotions were on edge day after day. Were we totally crazy? I know a lot of our friends and family must have thought so.

Backing Up a Little

We had already given up our security, back in 1997, in Raymond, Washington, where we had started a church and Christian School in 1983. We had kept that tough work going for over fourteen years.

I had been working for most of that time in the local community hospital as a surgical tech. I had benefits, plus pay for being on call 24 hours a day most of the time, and pretty decent wages. Ben was running the church and the Christian school. Our family income and financial security were at an all-time high, when suddenly the Lord was asking us to leave it all behind and move to Spokane for some reassignment in His Kingdom. At that time we had thought that we might be preparing for some missionary evangelism in the Yucatan region of Mexico.

Now two years later, after spending one year in intensive prophetic schooling in Spokane and other locations, and the second year in helping Ken and Valencia start Covenant Faith Center, we were doing something even crazier than what we did when we left Raymond.

Launching Out

Without any medical insurance and without any church or private support, we were taking our family of four and heading for Chicago. After a few short weeks in Illinois, we would head back west into Alberta, Canada, for a ladies retreat and a few church and home meetings.

After that we would spend most of the winter in the San Diego area. Our daughter, Barbie, with her husband Caleb, had headed to Tijuana, Mexico, for their own faith adventure. We would find a location as close as possible to them, and try to help them in some way with their missionary work. We also hoped that God would open some new doors for meetings which hopefully would help pay our bills. The bills didn't seem to go away, even though our regular income had. Of course, knowing that Barbie was expecting her second baby in January, we had even more reason to be in San Diego.

Finally, after weeks of making decisions and working like crazy, we took what we could fit into the van and trailer and headed for Chicago. As we left Spokane, early in

September 1999, tears began to flow. The boys were still not emotionally prepared to leave everything behind and I wasn't either. But I had to think of enough happy things to get their minds off of what they were leaving behind. It wasn't easy, but we slowly transitioned into preparing for the future and leaving the past behind. We knew that we had heard from God and could not turn back.

Chicago and Calgary

The meetings in Chicago were very blessed and many new doors opened while we were there. We had done mostly home meetings and very few churches, but more pastors began to attend the home meetings and then invite us to their churches. We had already made a lot of friends in Chicagoland and we were beginning to develop better relationships with many of them while also meeting new people all the time. Some of these folk would end up blessing us in so many ways that we could never have predicted. One open door led to another and although we experienced a major attack there which was designed to squelch our ministry in Chicago, it has continuously expanded in every direction.

After about three weeks in Illinois, we let our friends know we would be back in the Spring and headed for beautiful Calgary, Alberta, in western Canada, close to the Canadian Rockies. There I would speak the second time at a ladies retreat sponsored by the Full Gospel churches of that area. After that we would minister in a couple of church meetings and a home meeting or two.

The Smiths

As usual, we were given a warm welcome by our Canadian friends. Ben was raised in Canada, and we had gotten to know Robert and Ellen Smith when we pastored a Christian and Missionary Alliance church in Parry, Saskatchewan. The Smiths pastored an Apostolic Church in neighboring Pangman, and we had done some meetings together in their church with our former pastor and mentor, Elmer Burnette. Now they had opened some doors for us and invited us to speak in their church in West Calgary.

When I first met Pastor Smith, I didn't know how to take him and his sense of humor. He could say the most serious sounding things with a straight face, while all the time he was just kidding me. The Smiths were always lots of fun and we had babies about the same time. In fact, our Barbie and their Carolyn were dedicated at the same time by Brother Burnette, when he was in Saskatchewan for special meetings.

Thanks to the doors opened by the Smiths, we have been coming back to Alberta once or twice a year and have made many friends and ministered in many different churches. In fact at this writing, they have had me speak at six different ladies retreats in two different locations. In addition, we have ministered in about a dozen different churches and a couple of camps in Alberta in the last few years, because they were willing to take a risk with us and open other doors for us.

CHAPTER TWO

Just Deal With It

When we started ministering in various places, my favorite saying was "Just deal with it!" I had lots of crazy stories to tell of my own adventures (which keep on coming), and I used them to tell everyone we spoke to that "stuff" happens and we had better learn to "just deal with it."

Let me tell you now without any hesitation that I was speaking from experience. I was completely out of my comfort zone. There was no way that I had ever dreamed that I would be placed in front of about 20,000 or more individuals in the first five years and asked to give them a word from God. And I had certainly never thought about just how romantic it would be to travel in an R. V. for those five years, living in such crowded quarters with three guys and no female companions.

From the beginning, I had to learn to "deal with it". My flesh rebelled many times at the lifestyle that God had called us to. Fear of criticism from Christians who didn't understand my heart, and panic attacks that would almost paralyze me before meetings had to be overcome on a regular basis. I had frequent recurring thoughts: "What if God doesn't show up? And what if He's mad at me for my stupid flesh mistakes?" These thoughts kept me on my face before God. I had no problem encouraging others, but I did seem to have a problem receiving the frequent encouraging words that others spoke to me.

But day after day, I determined to "deal with it" and go on. Later, God would bring more people across my path who would pray off of me some of the attacks from the enemy. I am so thankful for each of these "divine encounters" that helped me move into a greater freedom and joy in serving Jesus.

Van on Fire

After one of our first trips to Chicago from Spokane, we were headed home with our Chevy van, towing our 33 foot trailer. Suddenly, we noticed smoke coming from under the van. This had happened once before when our transmission had overheated and spilled out fluid, which made a lot of smoke. Ben figured that it was happening again and quickly pulled over. He knew that we had a major problem and that our schedule was going to be interrupted by some down time for repairs.

What neither of us knew was that the transmission fluid was not only making smoke, but the heat from the transmission had started it on fire. As soon as we got out and looked under the van, we could see the flames. I grabbed the boys and got them out of the car as fast as I possibly could while Ben grabbed a small fire extinguisher out of the trailer. But when he tried to extinguish the fire, the fire extinguisher extinguished itself after spraying for about two seconds. It hadn't put a dent in the fire.

Meanwhile, a trucker had pulled up parallel to us ready to merge onto the freeway we were on. He could see not only the smoke, but also the fire. He grabbed his larger fire extinguisher and hustled over and quickly put out the flames. It was like being "Touched by an Angel", because as soon as the fire was out, he was back in his truck and down the freeway. We never got his name or phone number, but we hope to see him in Heaven so we can thank him again for saving our vehicles from being incinerated.

Both the van and the trailer had to be towed into town by separate tow trucks. The van went to the shop which miraculously had time to work on it right away. The trailer was towed to an R. V. park, where we took time to relax a day or two, while a new transmission, along with a temperature gauge, was being installed in the van.

God had protected us and shown His loving care in so many ways. The van had caught on fire just outside Sioux Falls, South Dakota, just before a long a stretch where there aren't any cities. And not only were we near a good-sized city, but we had pulled over right by an on-ramp, which made it easy for the trucker to pull over when he saw our dilemma. And the timing was so perfect, because according to the mechanic, we could have had an explosion any minute or even any second, because the fire was burning wires and could have hit the gas line so quickly. In addition, we couldn't have disconnected the trailer from the van, and the trailer could have caught fire as well if there had been a gas tank explosion.

Our insurance covered some of the expenses and my parents helped us with the rest so we could get the van running again and return to Washington. We spent a couple of days in South Dakota with a loaner car and saw some of the sights, including a museum, which we all enjoyed. We hadn't planned on the fire but God helped us to "Deal with it", and soon we were back on the road again. I was learning quickly the lesson that "God is so God!"

Rattled by a Snake in Central Washington

Another experience in those early days actually happened when we were visiting family between meetings. My parents' home in Soap Lake was near the edge of that small town, not far from some rolling hills in this semi-desert region of central Washington. We had parked our new motor home (the trailer had been worn out by then) in front of their house. I was carrying out a large round bowl from the house to the motor home.

Walking down the middle of the sidewalk in front of their house, I was prompted to look down over the large bowl that I was carrying. Instantly, I saw a large rattle snake, fully coiled, and sticking out his tongue at me. I have heard that when you see a snake, you should stand still like a tree, but this grandma had no intentions of pretending that she was a tree. Instead, the bowl went flying, while I somehow flew straight backwards with my sandals staying just one foot from the snake. Still in shock, I ran into the house.

When I caught my breath, I looked out the window to see that unwelcome reptile still coiled and still sticking out his tongue. I knew he was thinking, "Now where did she go?" My dad and Ben ran out with a shovel to try to kill it, but it slithered away into the thick shrubbery. When that happened, my dad was afraid that the snake would kill their poodle, Peppy. A day or two later they found a 28 inch rattler resting in the basement window well. It was no doubt the same snake as I had encountered. Somehow they disposed of it.

Had I not looked down at the precise moment I did, I would have been right on top of that snake. I know he was not really out to get me, but he would have certainly struck at me in self defense. I have always hated snakes, spiders and bees of all kinds, but snakes would be number one on my list of things that I wish to have nothing to do with. But as always, God was with me and I could say again, "God is so God!"

Blowout on a Snowy Mountain Road

On our way to Calgary, Alberta, we were traveling through beautiful British Colombia in late October. We were going through some mountains in our motor home near a beautiful lake. The road was mostly bare but the narrow shoulder was covered with snow. Coming around a curve on a narrow two-lane highway, Ben saw an object that looked like a block of wood. With cars and trucks coming in the other lane he was not able to avoid hitting it with the right front tire.

For a quarter mile or so nothing happened, but suddenly the tire blew and Ben quickly guided the motor home as far off the road as possible. Unfortunately, we were still sticking out somewhat onto the highway. Not only that, we were on a hill and semis and cars were whizzing past us, using both lanes to avoid hitting us. And not only that, it was getting dark. Needless to say, I was in a panic/prayer mode.

Ben had never changed a tire on the motor home and it's a lot harder than a car. Getting the spare out of its storage compartment was a challenge and getting the flat off was another. Meanwhile trucks of all sizes were barreling down the hill at the same time as others were climbing towards us from below. I knew that if two big rigs went by us at the same time from opposite directions, we were in big trouble.

After struggling for almost a half hour, Ben was making a little progress, but was having some major problems with the job of getting the tire loose. As I continued to cry out to our Heavenly Father for mercy, God did a miracle for us.

Suddenly we saw flashing yellow lights behind us coming toward us. It was a Highway snowplow truck. Seeing us there, he parked behind us, leaving his lights flashing to warn the vehicles coming down the hill. Then he added his knowledge, experience and physical strength to Ben's, and quickly had the tire changed. Soon we were back on the road again. When we got to Calgary, we were able to purchase new tires and once again see God touch many people with encouragement and healing. And once again I could say, "God is SO God!"

Failing Forward

Early in our travels, our son, Ken, who is currently a pastor in Spokane, handed me a book by John Maxwell, entitled, "Failing Forward". I had to get over the idea that he was implying that I had been a failure, which I already felt I had been in a lot of ways. But he encouraged me it was about leadership and would be a real blessing to me.

Ken was right. I learned so much from this book and a few others similar to it. I not only learned the principles for myself, but I have been able to teach many others the same principles and I often recommend the book to others as well. I have actually given away a number of my own personal copies, so that my husband has to keep buying me new ones.

It's sad but so many of us have been raised with a victim mentality. We never want to take the blame or responsibility for anything. If something goes wrong, we always want to find someone else to blame. I had a hard time with guilt and condemnation and would always want to find a reason not to accept more guilt. I have an emotional personality and have not always kept it under control, and the devil would always harass me about my past failures. Instead of accepting those failures and receiving forgiveness, my natural tendency would be to justify my failures by blaming others.

I discovered the principle of taking responsibility for my own actions. Earlier in my adult life, I had been taught how to ask forgiveness through a well know seminar which we attended several times. But like many children growing up with several siblings, I would instinctively want to blame someone or something else when something went wrong, so as not to get punished. I would wrestle with the guilt and instinctive fear of the consequences by trying to pass the responsibility and blame onto others. Now I try to accept the responsibility and then accept the forgiveness. I've had to learn that no one else is to blame for my actions. And of course, no one is to blame for your actions but you.

You have probably told someone at some time, "You make me so mad!" That's really not true. If someone can "make" you mad, then they have power over you. No one can make you mad; you actually choose to get mad. No one can make you jealous; it's your choice. And no one can make you happy if you chose not to be. It's time for all of us to take responsibility for our actions and admit that we have failed, but let's use our failures to learn and grow. That's how you "Fail Forward."

I have been failing forward for several years now. It has helped me to work with all the members of our family and others that we spend time with. The things I have learned have hopefully helped thousands of others as we have had the privilege of speaking in so many places here in North America and South Korea.

This is the principle that I apply when orange juice gets spilled (that story is in a later chapter) and other things happen. I know that I still fail many times, but I know that I can fail forward and let Jesus help me to grow in His grace.

Like everyone else, I inherited tendencies, both positive and negative. The negative tendencies included anger and self-pity. Both of these can be very damaging to both myself and those around me. I didn't want to pass these on to my children any more than I already had. I decided early on in our ministry that I would do whatever it took to stop these family tendencies from being passed on to future generations.

Over the years I humbled myself repeatedly and got prayer from various ministries and cried out to God for victory. I responded to almost every altar call available that related to my weaknesses. Today, what I do most is take time to soak in His presence (next chapter). During soaking times, I feel the negative attitudes leaving me and giving me peace. This is what works best for me and I highly recommend it to you, along with changing your mind set to accept the responsibility and your failures in order that you can "Fail Forward".

By the way, if you have an emotional personality like I do, and if you struggle with some strong negative emotions, you might be interested in a book written by my husband, Ben. It's called, "Go Ahead, Be So Emotional!" He first of all reveals what a blessing your emotional personality can be to the Kingdom of God, and then gives some wisdom for minimizing your negative emotions and maximizing your positive emotions. The book includes God's Emotional Hall of Fame, and how emotions have gotten an unfair bad rap in our society and in the church.

CHAPTER 3

Learning to Soak

E arly on in our faith journey, God bestowed on me a very special blessing in the form of a compact disk entitled, "Paradise Is Waiting" by a young musician named Scott Brenner. We had never met him, but a pastor at Pal Bok Korean Presbyterian Church in Vernon Hills, Illinois, gave me the CD and encouraged me to listen to it. Right away, it did something for me that almost nothing else did. It began to take me into the presence of God in a deeper way than I had ever known before.

The Cross at Indian Hills Camp

We spent our first two winters in the San Diego area, while our oldest daughter, Barbie and her husband, Caleb, were missionaries in Tijuana, Mexico. Near the town of Jamul, California, not far from San Diego, there is a wonderful ministry called Indian Hills Camp. They were so gracious to give us a place to park our trailer without charge. In appreciation, Ben, who had been a house painter while getting started in ministry, did several paint jobs for them and I also helped in the camp where I could.

This was a camp which ministered to many kids every year. With the warm climate you could have camps running year round. During school time, many kids came on field trips to enjoy the western setting and the little "kids zoo" they had, which included a couple of donkeys, numerous rabbits, rats and mice of various kinds, exotic chickens, waterfowl and many other creatures. They also had a reptile room with many snakes and lizards, etc.

The history of the camp was very interesting. God had directed a missionary, whose husband had died on the mission field, to come home and invest her life and substance into a Christian camp for kids. They had built three crosses on a hill near the chapel. They had used them for passion plays. These crosses remained there until a wild forest fire, fanned by the famous Santa Anna winds, roared towards the camp. Great prayer went up for the camp and it was totally spared. The only casualties on the entire camp grounds were two of the crosses on the hill. The middle cross, which represented the cross of Jesus, was still standing tall and untouched by the flames, but the other two were burned. For the camp staff, that surviving center cross had a special meaning, reminding them of the protection that God had provided during the time of extreme danger.

While we stayed in California and while I was anticipating the challenge of ministry that was waiting for me in the coming months in the Chicago area, I would get so anxious and stressed about the responsibility that I would get up early almost every morning and take my portable CD player and CD up the hill to the cross. There I would pour out my heart to the Lord and let the tears roll down my cheeks onto the dirt at the foot of the cross.

After an hour or two with God, I would feel the comfort of the Holy Spirit and return to my family. I will never forget those encounters with Jesus there at the foot of that cross that wouldn't burn. It was during those hours with Him that He was able to do spiritual surgery on my whole being. I knew I had a lot of baggage from my past and I could feel my load getting lighter as I spent more and more time soaking in the presence of Jesus.

Before we left Spokane to travel full time, I had started taking my music into the bathroom when I wanted to take a bath. Sometimes it was the only way I could get away from everyone and just soak in the presence of Jesus, while I was physically soaking in the tub. I actually began to use the term "soaking" because I was soaking in the tub and transferred it to the concept of soaking in His presence. It was not a term I had heard from any other sources at the time.

Soaking in Toronto

A month or two later, I was invited to go to Toronto, Canada, for a conference where Heidi Baker was speaking. Her message powerfully impacted my life, but the most impacting thing of all was a workshop that was just called, "Soaking". I had never heard anyone else really talking about soaking and I had never heard a workshop on the subject in all my days as a pastor's wife, so I decided to check it out.

The place for this workshop was a large room where people were encouraged to just relax and listen. Some were sitting, but probably most were lying on the floor and absorbing the presence of God. Wonderful worship teams came in and ministered for a period of time and then another team would come in to replace them. We were told to just rest our minds and invite God to come.

Very quickly, I felt the presence of God coming to me. It was such an enriching experience that I wanted to keep doing it even more after I left Toronto. My Scott Brenner CD was the perfect tool for me to use wherever we happened to be. Sometimes it was in the back of our trailer or motor home, but other times it was at the front of a church where we were parked.

A year and a half later or so, we attended a conference in Chicago where Scott Brenner was leading worship. We got to meet him and plan a conference with him, which we held a few months later. It was a glorious experience and such a privilege to have him leading worship as well as speaking at our packed-out conference. The theme for that conference was "A Passion For the Father's Heart." It was during the conference that we found out that Scott was actually an attorney, who had left his law practice to join the twenty-four hour houses of prayer in Kansas City and practice the presence of Jesus. That was when God gave him much of his original music, which is now helping many others like myself enjoy the glory of God's presence.

After our first encounter with Scott, we were privileged

to carry his CDs with us to sell in our meetings. Since then hundreds of people have begun to enjoy the same anointing as they listen to Scott's CDs.

By the way, Heidi Baker has become a very special example to us and we have had the privilege of hearing her again recently in a conference in Canada. What God is doing through her and her husband is totally amazing, but we know they are called to model what the church is to become in these exciting days of harvest before the Lord returns.

Physical Healing

There were times in those years when I was in considerable physical pain. One time we were parked in a church parking lot and we were given a key to the church. I would go early in the morning and lay at the front of the church with my soaking music. I had some severe pain in my back and neck, which was really bothering me. While crying out for Him to touch me, I felt the pain leave my body. I left that church that morning, knowing that I had soaked up His healing virtue.

Another time more recently, I was suffering from a broken rib. It was not my first broken rib experience and I knew that under normal circumstances it would be very painful for many weeks and gradually get better. But this time, although it was not as painful at the beginning, it had gotten worse than ever before. Because of my years in surgery (I was an O. R. Tech), I knew that something serious could be happening, such as a vital organ near the rib being punctured by a splintered rib. In our busy schedule, we had not taken time to get an X-Ray and I was getting very concerned and not at all enjoying the excruciating pain.

I went to the back of the motor home and closed the thin veneer door. I turned my music up and cried out to the Lord for His mercy and His healing power. We had a very busy schedule ahead of us in the Chicago area and I told God that I just couldn't do it unless He touched me.

Suddenly, I saw a light that had entered my room. Then a cross appeared in the light. The power of the cross of Jesus was poured out onto my body. My rib snapped into place and the intense pain left immediately. I had been healed again in the presence of Jesus. Only a slight tenderness remained to remind me that my rib had been broken. I never missed a meeting because of that broken rib.

Teaching Others to Soak

I was getting invited to speak at ladies' retreats, Aglow meetings and other meetings with Ben. I wasn't a theologian or Bible teacher, so I just shared what was touching my own life. Soaking was the biggest thing in my life, so I began to share about soaking everywhere I spoke.

In Hanna, Alberta, after I ministered separately to the women, a lady from the church asked me if I could teach her how to soak. I told her that it was not really that complicated, but if she wanted, she could come to soak with me the next morning at about 6 A.M. She happened to mention it to a couple of other gals. At 6:00 o'clock she and several others showed up including one of the husbands.

I instructed them to lie down on the carpet on their

backs and not look around. I put on "Paradise is Waiting", and lay down with them. Soon I could hear the sweet sound of soft weeping. I knew Jesus had come to visit these hungry hearts. I hadn't done anything but lay down with them on the floor and put on the music. The Holy Spirit had done the rest and He had revealed the presence of Jesus to them. That was the beginning of teaching others like I had been taught.

Later, I was the speaker at a ladies' retreat at the Enthios Retreat Center near Calgary, Alberta. I announced to the one hundred or so gals that I would be coming to soak at about 6 A.M. I had no idea how many would show up at that early hour. At 5:00 o'clock I could hear a rustle and bustle of activity. Showers were going in almost every room. By 6:00 o'clock most of the ladies were in the sanctuary with blankets and pillows. Again, the sweet presence of Jesus filled the sanctuary and prepared the atmosphere for a powerful day of encounters with God.

I had invited ladies from Chicago and Washington to join me at the retreat to help minister to the Alberta ladies. Three came from Chicago and two came from Washington, including Sherelen Bryant, an anointed soloist that I knew from Raymond, the town where we had pastored for almost fifteen years. All five of these ladies were taken to a new level in their own ministries. I figured that since God was stretching me and making me walk on the water and step off a cliff every night, then that's what He wanted to do with them as well. The results were just awesome!

That same Saturday, after a powerful day in the presence of the Lord, we were in for a Holy Spirit explosion. It was something that no one could have planned. During the preliminaries a retreat staff member reminded all the ladies that they should have put their bed sheets, etc. in the hall outside their rooms, and if anyone had forgotten they needed to go back now. I realized that I had forgotten to complete that little assignment in my busyness. So there I was, in front of all the ladies, walking out to do my little chore. They all had a good laugh at my expense.

But God had a divine appointment all planned for me. On the way back to my dorm room I saw a deer very close to me. It did something I had never seen before. It jumped straight up and down several times before it bounded away. Right then the Holy Spirit spoke to me. "That's what you will do tonight." I was quickly reminded of another Scott Brenner CD that had an appropriate song for jumping.

That night, after I shared some things on my heart, I invited Lori Johnson, a young pastor's wife from Strathmore, Alberta, to come up with me and do something that I would never have done in front of over one hundred women. We put on the CD and began to jump to the music. We invited everyone to do the same. Soon everyone was loosened up and having a great time. From that point on, God broke in on the scene and people began to be overcome by the presence of God. Some were laughing, some were crying, some were on the floor and many were speaking prophetically into each others lives. It was a Holy Ghost blowout like I have seldom seen.

We began ministering to people again in teams, while everything else was going on. So many lives were impacted that only eternity will reveal what was accomplished. Even the most sophisticated ladies among us were totally overcome and swept along into the river of God. It was a long night of celebration and ministry that none of us will ever forget. Almost everyone was ministering to someone or being ministered to. What was so powerful about the whole thing was that it wasn't about Brenda, it was about the Holy Spirit and many gals were participating in the ministry.

It was an awesome day, but I don't really think that we would have had the powerful results we witnessed if the people hadn't prepared their hearts by soaking in the presence of God earlier in the day. The atmosphere had been established then and was enhanced as the day progressed. By evening it was so charged with "Heavenly electricity" that something was going to happen, regardless of what I spoke about.

The Autopsy

When I teach on soaking, I usually mention the autopsy I was required to watch while taking my training as an O.R. Technician in Regina, Saskatchewan. This was a bit of a traumatic experience for many students who were training with me. I was warned that the fragrance in the room might not exactly be like Evening in Paris or Channel #5. I took the advice of a friend and spread Noxzema ointment on my O.R. mask. It kept me from smelling the unpleasant odor of the formaldehyde.

But the part of the whole autopsy that was the most fascinating was when they examined the brain. First, the head was literally scalped and then the skull was opened up with a special skill saw. Then the brain was removed and placed on a cutting board. Finally, a big knife was used to chop the brain up in slices like a big piece of cheese, so that it could be examined for abnormalities or blood clots.

After examining the brain, it was scooped up and placed back in a big black bag with all of the other internal organs. It was an amazing thing to watch. Now my mind always goes back to that scene. If we could just take out our brain and chop it up and stop thinking, we might be a lot better off. I have told hundreds of people over the years, "You think too much." It's not that God can't use our brains for His glory, but sometimes we just can't listen well because we are so busy thinking all the time and trying to figure God out, instead of waiting in silence, just listening for the still small voice of God.

So many people find it hard to be silent before God. We always feel like we should be praying or worshipping or something. But sometimes God is saying, "Be still and know that I am God." I know that there are also many other scriptures that use the word, "silent," in reference to waiting on God.

CHAPTER 4

Korea

Our friend, Matt Lee, associate pastor of Pal Bok Presbyterian Church of Vernon Hills, Illinois, told us that he
and Pastor Ha, the senior pastor, were going to send us to
South Korea. I wasn't too sure that I really wanted to go to
Korea, since I didn't know what to expect or how we would
communicate with anyone. It would also mean leaving
our two sons behind for three weeks or so.

Our daughter Barbie, with whom they would have to
stay, was living in Tijuana, Mexico. They were not exactly
living in the most exclusive apartments in Mexico. In fact
they had moved to a much poorer community after having
been put down by their middle class neighbors for bringing
in some of the people who were living in the slums across a
garbage-filled ravine. Barbie had visited many of them and
led several of them to the Lord and brought them to their
church. They really loved her and wanted to come to visit. It
so bothered her that the middle class people in the apartments,

where they lived, were so prejudiced against the poor.

So Caleb and Barbie had moved into some very low-class apartments where drugs and crime were quite common. The playground was just dirt and broken glass and was no place for children who liked to play outside. Barbie's kids were still babies, and our boys were about ten and twelve. But Barbie was such a great sister to them and always willing to help out. She knew the boys would be fine, even though they didn't speak Spanish. There was a market not far away and a few kids from their church lived in the same apartments.

Well, it wasn't long until we were headed for Seoul, South Korea, leaving the boys behind in Tijuana. It was to be a real life adventure for me. I had never left North America before, except for a short trip to Hawaii, where I had met Ben on his way home from India. Ben had traveled a lot when our first three were small, but I had stayed home with them. Traveling into Tijuana was plenty scary enough for me. But we were about to embark on one of the greatest and most intense adventures of our lives.

Surprises Begin

We had been told that we would be doing our School of Prophetic Ministry starting on Monday night. We arrived on Saturday night with severe jet-lag, an eight hour change in time. We were picked up for church on Sunday, thinking that we would sit and observe the Korean church in action. We were ushered into the office where the pastor spoke to us through a highly educated interpreter, who was president of Global University in Korea and a pastor with five or six associate pastors.

The pastor informed Ben that he was to preach that morning. That was the first surprise. The next surprise came on Monday night (after a wonderful day of sight-seeing) when the interpreter told us the agenda for the service. First we preach, then we "knock them down", and then we prophesy. I turned to Ben and said, "But we don't have a knock'em-down ministry." He just said, "Let's not worry about it now." That was easier said than done.

After we both had shared what was on our hearts, we were asked to lay hands on all the pastors and leaders first. There were about twenty or more that came up on the large platform. As we prayed for them, they began to experience the powerful presence of God and almost all fell backwards with catchers laying them down in a somewhat orderly fashion. Then they lined up the whole congregation, perhaps two hundred or more. One by one they responded to the laying on of hands and went down to soak up a little more of the presence of God. This was to become a normal routine in all four churches where we ministered in South Korea.

This phenomenon was not a result of us being so anointed; rather it was the result of these people having spent so much time in prayer and in soaking in the presence of God that they were extremely sensitive to the moving of His Spirit. They loved to feel His presence and they had an expectation that since we had come from such a distance, we must surely be carriers of great anointings. After that time of "knocking them down", we were led into the pastor's lovely office, where we were seated on a comfortable couch with a coffee table in front of us. They always provided us with refreshments such as fruit and the ever-present ginseng drink to keep us going. Across the coffee table was another couch where the people who wanted ministry would sit. Then they began to bring them in, one or two at a time. It seemed to us they were bringing the people off the streets, there were so many every meeting.

From that point on our schedule was so intense, I wonder how we did it. Most days had meetings morning, afternoon and evening. People had signed up for personal prophecy for who knows how long. We got so tired, but somehow we kept going. We went three full weeks without a day off except for traveling between cities. Somehow God kept us going. I think it was being so continuously in the presence of God that kept us energized. Of course, the ginseng helped too.

From the beginning of our time in Korea we fell in love with these precious and resilient people, who had suffered so much over the centuries at the hands of powerful neighbors and even their own governments. The people we met were incredibly passionate about their love for Jesus. They had a tradition of spending hours in prayer and soaking in the presence of God. Their worship was powerful and truly awesome and they weren't afraid to dance before the Lord and express their emotions in His presence.

Pul Gogi

They treated us like royalty the whole time we were with them. They fed us the very best they had to offer in the best restaurants. Pul Gogi was a meal we had many times. It means "fire meat" or "fire beef". It was like an indoor barbeque with the fire pit in the middle of the table. Pieces of beef were cut in strips and laid on the grill. Many other delicacies were added to the fire. Dozens of little bowls with various new and strange looking items were placed on the table around the fire pit.

Plates with various edible leaves were also placed on the table. These leaves became the tortillas in which we would wrap the small pieces of beef, dipped in delicious sauces, along with other delicacies. Of course, we used chop sticks to pick up each item to put into the leaves. Then the trick was to get it all into your mouth without spilling it all out. I tried to be lady-like and bite half of the bundle, but that turned out to be a disaster. It all fell apart and back into my little bowl. The Koreans were so polite and pretended not to notice. I learned that you had to make it small enough to get the whole thing into your mouth. By the way, a full mouth was O.K., but if you needed to pick your tooth with a tooth pick, proper etiquette requires that you cover your mouth with the other hand.

One of my first social blunders happened when our tour guide, a precious Korean lady, who spoke almost no English, took us out to eat our first meal in Korea at a very fancy restaurant. The servers placed many little bowls on the table close to our little plate or bowl. I thought that there was only one of each kind, so I began to pass the little bowls to our Korean guide. She graciously accepted the first two or three and then held up her hand and shook her head.

There were at least two of each item and the servers had

placed one of each close enough to each person. There was no need to pass anything. You just reached as far as you had to in order to get what you needed. Long chopsticks helped of course to reach a little farther. Of course, using chopsticks is not my specialty, especially the stainless steel kind that most Koreans use. They are much more slippery to use than wooden ones, and I often lost my little item into another bowl on the way to my bowl or my mouth.

The Wedding Dress

As I said, we were treated like royalty and we were shown love in such powerful ways. One of the highlights of the first trip was the time we spent in Kwang Ju in southern Korea. It was a city that had experienced some terrible things just a decade or two earlier. There had been a protest against some government policies. The army had come in and put down the protest with incredible cruelty, killing many people, including totally innocent women and children. The people believed that the soldiers had been given drugs to remove their inhibitions. There was still a spirit of grief on the whole city. The stories we heard were so terrible that my heart broke when I heard them.

The church in Kwang Ju also functioned as a Bible College and we came to teach the students about the prophetic. I know they taught us at least as much as we taught them. This was another group that loved to dance before the Lord and they insisted that I joined in with them. Actually, they came and got me and pulled me into their joyful celebration. We had so much fun in the presence of the Lord. It changed my idea of what church was supposed to be like.

Before our last service with this awesome group we were taken into the pastor's little living quarters. The pastor's wife pulled out a traditional Korean wedding dress. She insisted that she wanted to give it to me. I had a hard time letting her do it. Koreans often have two wedding dresses. One is a modern style wedding dress, but they also wear a traditional oriental dress for a different part of the celebration and for photos. She had owned this dress for many years, and now she was going to part with it and send it across the Pacific Ocean, where she would never see it again. We all shed a few tears that night before the meeting.

They had also bought me a little girl's traditional Korean dress, which was extremely lovely. I brought back both of the dresses and used them in some of my ladies' meetings. I would always have others model them for me, while I talked about our time in Korea.

Team Massage

After a long service that night in Kwang Ju, knowing we were quite exhausted, the leaders asked us to lay ourselves face-down on the platform. Then several people began to massage our bodies in various places, including our feet. It was a bit humbling and even a bit painful at times as they were quite aggressive in their massaging. But they knew exactly what they were doing and our muscles were much more relaxed when we left their city.

Korea – The Second Time Around

One year later in 2001, we found ourselves back in South Korea again. The only problem this time was that our meetings were scheduled to start one week after the terrorist attack of 9-11. All flights were grounded after the attack, and we were filled with uncertainty as we waited for the doors to open. The big church in Seoul had spent over $1000.00 advertising our meetings, which were to begin in their church. We finally had to tell them we wouldn't make it for their first week of meetings. The Seoul church lost the advertising money, but we did minister in their church our last week in Korea instead of the first week.

We finally got to Seoul about a week late. We were totally wiped out after almost no sleep the night before, and then many hours flying from Seattle to San Francisco and then on to Seoul. We were looking forward to a long night's sleep in our motel to get ready for the first meetings the next day, which was Sunday.

But that was not going to happen! In broken English we were told that we were going straight to a church for our first meeting. The church wanted us for Saturday night, Sunday morning and Sunday night. It was in a city not far from Seoul, so after a long car ride, we began a crusade in a church that was brand new to us.

But God is so God and He showed up in spite of our exhaustion. Many people were touched in obvious ways as tears flowed and great joy was manifested. The worship was so special and sincere that we were lifted out of our exhaustion and into the presence of God. The blessings continued the next day and in every church we visited.

Adventures in Pusan

One of the most exciting things that happened on our second trip to Korea was going to a small church ministry in Pusan, a city in southeast Korea. We totally fell in love with the pastor and his wife and their drama and worship team. Such intense worship we had seldom witnessed. Many of the young people who ministered so powerfully had been abused or abandoned as children. The pastor and his wife had discipled them and taught them to do drama, worship and dance. They even did a couple of dramas in English. We were so incredibly blessed to experience the anointing they released through the arts.

These young people were so intense in their worship of Jesus that it was exhilarating just to watch them. Often, they would dance before the Lord with incredible energy for perhaps an hour and then fall suddenly to the floor and lay motionless as if in a trance for a long period of time.

The pastor and his wife still call us Father and Mother, and we hear from them every now and then. We really wanted to bring them and their team to North America, but nothing has worked out yet.

We missed our scheduled flight back to Seoul for the conclusion of our three week tour, so we were able to go to the regular evening prayer meeting in Pusan. What an awesome time we had! The fact is that I cried through the entire prayer meeting. God's presence was just so powerful because of their broken, humble spirit. We didn't preach or teach. We just prayed with these precious people and received a blessing from God with them.

Seoul

We finally got back to Seoul the next morning and then started our meetings in the big church in this city of 12 million souls. We had a wonderful time again with the leaders and the people we had met the year before. The worship was powerful and again we were brought into a spirit of celebration with beautiful and joyful dancing before the Lord.

Again, we spent hours ministering one-on-one in the pastor's office. We ministered to hundreds of eager Koreans and met some very special people. We were always treated like royalty and were introduced to many who were considered "important people". For us all of the people were special, and we know that they are all special to God.

Final Korean Adventure

We were often taken out to dinner in very exclusive restaurants. Some were in beautiful and expensive hotels. Their custom was for one person or couple to pay for all the guests, which included pastors and other leaders. Ben, who was considered the most worthy guest in the group, would be given the name of the person or couple who was paying the bill. He was then asked to pray for specific requests that the person or couple had, which might include a desire for a husband or wife or a blessing on their business.

Before our last night in Seoul we were taken to a very expensive hotel and treated to a very special meal. We found out that the lady who was paying for our meal owned a cell phone company. Ben noticed that the Korean cell phone we had rented when we landed at the airport was rented from her company. Her brother, who was also with us, owned a business in Japan. During the meal, she asked me if I would like a Korean massage.

After asking a few questions, I agreed to her offer. Her answers were only partly true as I would soon discover. I had absolutely no idea what I was getting into. This story is too personal to tell in detail the way I do when just ladies are present, but let me say that it was definitely one of the most intensely embarrassing experiences in my life.

After our final meeting the next night after our fancy dinner, we ministered until about 11 P.M. in the pastor's office. Several ladies, including the pastor's wife, were waiting for me to get done so they could take me to this very expensive, exclusive club where I would be introduced to a whole new concept in massage treatments.

After a long drive through this massive city, we arrived at the right location. For the next several hours I was baked, caked and scraped with various things. Some of it was physically painful, but what hurt the most was my pride. You will only get the details if you come to a ladies' meeting where I am speaking.

The conclusion however, was very precious. Because I was willing to submit to what they wanted to do for me, I experienced a deeper level of bonding with these precious ladies. Our stringy hair, lack of make-up, etc., left us without any external mask to cover our physical defects. And somehow, I felt the same reaction in the soul and spirit realm. Somehow, we felt closer to each other and there were some sincere hugs before we left the building sometime after 2:00 A.M.

Ben had just gone to sleep when I arrived home around 3:00 A.M. He had been worried about me, but had no way of finding out what happened to me so after spending time in prayer until he had peace that I was alright, he finally allowed himself to fall asleep. He awoke when I arrived and was so glad to see me safe and sound. He also noticed how smooth my skin was after all the treatments. I guess that was part of the purpose for the whole ordeal. Anyway, we were on our way to the airport by 7 or 8 A.M. the next morning.

The time had come to return to our boys who were again with Barbie and Caleb, but this time in Moses Lake, Washington. God had led Barbie and Caleb to return to Washington after two years in Mexico. They were working to establish a Spanish church, which is now a flourishing work in their small city.

Since we left Korea, we have received other invitations to come again, but we were not able to fit them into our schedule. Many times I have wondered if we'll ever go back again. My husband assures me that we will be back. He feels we have a calling from God to speak into the lives of church leaders there to prepare them for the days when North Korea will open up to the gospel.

CHAPTER 5

Finding Time for Fun

The kind of ministry we have been doing is very exhausting. Often we go night after night with meetings that may last until midnight or later. The intensity and responsibility of hearing accurately for words from God can drain all your strength, even though there is usually a surge of adrenalin while ministry is going on. But eventually, you usually get pretty exhausted. Sometimes you notice it the most the next morning.

At any rate, we have enjoyed some brief fun times along the way which have been a blessing to us and our boys. I have discovered that if we appreciate the little things God gives us, He is more likely to give us the bigger things down the road.

The Slide at Indian Hills Camp

The camp where we spent the first two winters of our traveling ministry had an awesome thirty foot slide. At the top was a great big tree-house and there was a ramp with steps to get to the top. Often on my way to the cross to soak in the presence of the Lord I would stop by the tree-house slide to get some exercise. This would be early in the morning before any campers would be out and about. I didn't want them watching this grandmother come shooting out of their tree-house slide.

I used the climb up to the tree-house as my physical exercise. I never seemed to get enough exercise to neutralize the calories I consumed, so I valued this early morning time to burn some of those calories. When I got to the top, the slide was my reward for the exercise. Depending on the material of your sweat pants, you could pick up a lot of speed coming down that slide. It was just one of those silly little fun things that made my day a little more interesting and I do thank God for it.

Birding with Fred and Marty

Ben's brother and sister-in-law, Fred and Marty Peters, had already retired and came camping with us in San Diego. They loved golf and bird-watching. Ben golfed once or twice with them while I worked on other projects. Trying to hit that little ball was not my idea of having fun, but I was somewhat fascinated with their love for bird-watching. I didn't really get into that myself, but Timothy and Nathan really took up the challenge of trying to identify as many birds as they could.

Uncle Fred bought them a birding book and a pair of binoculars. They quickly earned money to buy a second pair and later bought another pair or two. Then Fred and Marty took them to several sites to view some less common species. It became a great adventure for them in their preteen years and soon they had well over one hundred species viewed and identified.

Mount Rushmore

On one of our earliest trips to Chicago, we were able to stop and see the amazing sculptures at Mount Rushmore in South Dakota. We spent a few hours in the area viewing the history and taking pictures like typical tourists. We were on our way to a busy schedule in Illinois, but for the moment we were just enjoying what so many others had enjoyed on their family vacation.

Although my surgical technician job had some financial rewards, there had been one real negative attached. Because the hospital was so small, they didn't have many people who could fill in for me and they were all busy in their own positions. The result was that I was almost always on call and would have to ask far in advance for a day or two off to go anywhere out of town. I was virtually a prisoner to my beeper. I enjoyed the excitement of getting called in for a C-section or whatever, but when extended family or friends came to visit, and we wanted to go to the beach nearby, I would have to stay home.

Now there are many times I wish I could stay home but I'm thankful for the little blessings that I do get to enjoy, as well as the great blessing of knowing that God is using me to impact the lives of many people. I know that I don't really live down here. It's just another trip away from home, but someday we'll all be going home for good. I do look forward to that day.

Grand Canyon

We also found time to visit the Grand Canyon on our first trip into southwest Colorado for meetings in Cortez. We had just had our first ministry trip in Nevada. That had gone well and we didn't have a lot of time to waste on the road, but we did find time to spend a few hours looking over the canyon from different viewpoints.

We were once again impressed with the beauty of God's creation. It is an incredible view from anywhere, and pictures can't even come close to what you experience when you go there in person. As any mother would, I kept my eyes on my two adventurous sons, who would have liked to go as close to the edge as possible. Fortunately, no one fell into the canyon and we headed east and north to meet some folk in Cortez, Colorado.

Disneyland and Disneyworld

In the first five years of full-time traveling our family has been able to visit Disneyland twice and Disneyworld once. I love the excitement and fun of going with my kids and even my grandchildren. But in the five years of travel our sons have grown considerably and no longer are satisfied with the tamer rides. Timothy, at the time of this writing, is already sixteen and ready to try everything. And of course, he wants someone to ride with him. Nathan hasn't been quite as anxious to go on something that might make him feel sick, so Timothy is always asking Ben or me to go with him. I have gone on a few rides that I never would have chosen for myself, but I did survive them all and was able to help Timothy have a good time. Now Nathan is also able to handle the wilder rides and he accompanies Timothy on many of them. But once they have both been on a ride, they insist that Ben and I also try it. Again, sometimes I have to leave my comfort zone and try a new adventure or two.

Beaches in California and Florida

We haven't had a lot of time to just relax or take vacations, but we have had two or three times in Southern California near San Diego and in Florida where we could spend at least a half day at the beach and soak in some sun. I love to just walk along the shoreline and talk to Jesus. Sometimes Ben walks with me, and sometimes he watches the boys while I walk alone.

The boys and Ben have always loved the ocean and the beach. When we lived near the coast in Washington, we would get to the beach occasionally, but the water was extremely cold and the rip tides were dangerous. After several drownings there, people were not allowed to swim there any more. So the warmer beaches of San Diego and Tampa Bay were a lot of fun for all of us, and especially for me. As I mentioned earlier, I usually had to stay home when the family went to the beach in Washington, because the beach was too far away from our hospital in South Bend, where I was on call twenty-four hours a day most of the time.

CHAPTER 6

Life in an R.V.

Ben's Dream (Not Mine)

Ben had always dreamed of traveling with the family in a motor home. It had never been my dream. As I mentioned at the beginning, I didn't even like to camp. I like a house with a foundation that doesn't rock and roll when someone moves about or when the wind howls and shakes you as it often does in the suburbs of Chicago (the windy city) until you think your house is going to fall on its side.

When we started our journey four years ago, we had been given a thirty-three foot trailer. We also had been able to purchase a Chevy Van conversion to pull it with. It was a very nice ten year old trailer that had hardly been used and was quite beautiful. For a camping vehicle it was wonderful. Unfortunately, we weren't just camping. It was our home fifty-two weeks of the year.

Closet Space

We had about four feet of closet space, in which to put clothes for every occasion for four people. Do the math! Fortunately the boys could keep most of their clothes in tiny cupboards above the couch and table. However, it was still a struggle. There were times when we would be in meetings night after night and you needed a lot of dress clothes. Other times we would be with family or at a campground for a week or so, and you needed all casual clothes.

Then we were always changing seasons and we had to transition from summer clothes to winter clothes or *vice versa*. There was some storage space under the bed and in a few other places. There was almost no storage under the floor of the trailer like we now have in our motor home, which is called a basement model. Anyway, since we started this traveling life, Ben and I have had to constantly discipline ourselves to get rid of clothes that we weren't wearing, so we had some room for those we were wearing. The boys had to do the same. In the past, when we had a large house, we had always just left old clothes in the closet, thinking that some day we might wear them again.

Kitchen Space

The trailer had a little counter space but if you wanted to make a real meal and have a few people in for dinner, it was quite a chaotic mess trying to find room for everything. When we got the motor home, counter space was actually less than the trailer. Since the front of the motor home has the driving area, it couldn't be used for a counter the way the trailer was. Instead we have about a foot of counter space between the sink and the stove. The sink is a double sink, but both sinks are too narrow to hold a full-sized plate.

We found some light-weight plastic plates that do fit. We also have a small table with cushion bench seats, which can convert to a small bed. If the table isn't full of the boys' school work and various other things, you can also use it for counter space, but that is a rare thing.

I so miss being able to stick a turkey in the oven and make a holiday meal for our family in our own house. I usually help my mom or one of our married kids cook the turkey in their homes, but it's not the same.

The miniature refrigerator is another challenge. There is never enough room for everything. Things are stacked and jammed in to make them fit. As a result, opening the door can also be a dangerous experience, as items may end up on your toes, especially after moving the motor home. Of course that applies to all the cupboards and bathroom vanity.

Privacy (Or Lack of It)

We used to take for granted having a room to go to where we could close the door and have some real privacy. Our trailer had what I called a folding "paper" door. It was some kind of material but not much thicker than paper. It sealed off our "bedroom" from the rest of the trailer. It didn't seal out the sound or the shaking when someone moved around in the unit, but it was the only means of privacy in the whole trailer, outside of the little bathroom.

In the motor home we have a lightweight sliding veneer door, which is a little thicker, but still not noise proof. If we're not parked by a church where we have keys to get in the sanctuary, or somewhere else to go for privacy, I get a bit claustrophobic. I long for a place to get away to pray or sometimes just cry. Like most women, I feel so much better if I can let out the emotional buildup from stuff that happens. Sometimes I can go for a walk to pray and pour out my heart before the Lord. If the weather or the neighborhood restricts my walking, it is very hard for me to deal with being closed in. I usually find a reason to take off to the grocery store or a nearby Walmart, just to get away.

Living with three males in as much space as many people have in their kitchen or master bedroom, has been a challenge. Of course our bedroom is very small. For four years we have had no room to walk in our bedroom. The space at the sides is needed for storage, so the bed, itself, is the only place to park yourself in our bedroom. Our bathroom door in the motor home does open and blocks off the hall and closet area so that we have a "master bedroom" area. This is nice, but if the boys need to use the bathroom while I'm trying to get ready for a meeting, it creates a bit of stress.

As with the closets, we all have to be disciplined to do everything we need to do in the bathroom and dressing area and then get out to make room for the next person. I usually interrogate the boys and my husband before I begin to get ready. "Are you sure you don't need to get back in the bathroom or closet?" Usually someone does forget something and I have to deal with my irritation at being interrupted when I'm in a hurry trying to get my hair or my makeup done quickly, because we're running late.

Clobbered by a Tree

We hadn't had the trailer very long when we parked in a crowded trailer park on our way into Chicago for meetings. In the morning when we headed into the suburbs, Ben was watching an obstacle on the left, thinking he was O.K. on the right. But when he turned the van to the left, the back of the trailer swung out on the right side. A tree had a large branch leaning out on that side and put the squeeze on the back of the trailer.

It was heart-breaking! The back top corner was scrunched, the awning and the bedroom window both broke. We had insurance, but the repair shop didn't get the materials in time to fix a lot of it there before we left. They had the window shipped and Ben installed it in San Diego, but the dent remained and the inside of the trailer showed some damage as well. The rest of the insurance money was used to help us survive the winter financially and we had to live with the damage.

Soon the lower cabinets in that side (my side) of the bedroom were coming loose and other things started to deteriorate with all the traveling we did. In one stretch of road between Tulsa and Dallas the vibrations were so bad that we lost the cover to our battery and propane tank and the refrigerator stopped working. We got the insurance to help pay for those repairs, but little by little the trailer became less than ideal.

The Miracle of the Motor Home

Not only was the trailer deteriorating, but our van was also running out of steam. It used a lot of oil and required frequent repairs. When we returned from San Diego to Spokane in 2001, Ben said that he would not take the van and trailer on another trip across the mountains. We were already booked in Chicago a couple of weeks after we arrived in Spokane, so we all began to pray and shop for motor homes.

We finally found what we wanted; a brand new 2000, thirty-three foot Itasca that had sat on the lot for a year and had a factory-authorized price drop of $20,000. We had no cash, but we did own the trailer and they took that for a down payment. Getting the financing was still a major hassle as they didn't want to loan us that amount of money based on our unpredictable income and our income/debt ratio.

For several days we were on an emotional roller coaster ride. First it would look like we would get it. Then they found a problem and said, "Probably not." Several roadblocks were overcome before we finally took possession of the motor home. It really was a total miracle, because both our Credit Union and the dealership were willing to try some creative financing ideas that they had never done before.

We took possession about forty-eight hours before we had to be in Chicago for our first meeting. We still had about eighteen hundred miles to drive. We asked if we could cancel the first meeting, but it would be too hard to let people know, so we decided to go for it. Ben had only slept about three hours a night for the previous two nights because he was laying awake praying and trying to think of how to come up with the money to make the deal work. The next two nights on the road he also slept only three hours and then kept going. We rolled into Illinois about three hours before our first meeting. We parked near the church and got ready. It was a great meeting and after it was over we finally had a good sleep.

Timothy had just turned thirteen and Nathan was ten and a half. They both were so excited about the motor home that they couldn't stop saying, "Can you believe this is ours?" It was hard for all of us to believe. It was so new and clean and we could move around when we needed to. We could watch videos while we drove and we could get at the food in the kitchen.

We could even use the bathroom, which is one of the main reasons that Ben wanted a motor home instead of a trailer. He can drive for hours without stopping for a break, but some of us are not that gifted, and he would always have to stop so we could get into the trailer to use the bathroom. We could also sleep while he drove and he could get up in the middle of the night like he loved to do and just drive while we slept.

Another blessing was the generator. We could always have electricity if we needed it, by starting it up, as long as we had at least an eighth of a tank of gasoline or so. Whether we were parked or driving, we could make popcorn in the built-in microwave or use any other appliance we wanted to. Everything was so much better than before, but eventually we got used to the advantages and I guess, like many things in life, we began to take them for granted.

What Not To Do in a Motor Home

You don't want to boil water while you are driving, especially when you're in the city and you have to stop suddenly for traffic lights. The same goes for using the bathroom and putting on your pantyhose or any other operation that requires you to balance yourself on one leg.

While spending a little time in Dallas, Texas, our daughter, Andrea, was with us for a few days. We went shopping one day at a mall, a long way from where Andrea lived, at Christ For the Nations Institute, where we had been staying with our motor home. At that time we had no car with us and Andrea's car had broken down, so we had taken the motor home to the shopping center. Soon a Texas storm was whipping up and we were hearing a tornado warning for south Dallas, near where she lived. We chose to go to an R.V. park in the north end of Dallas, much closer to the mall.

While Ben was parking the motor home in the driving rain, Andrea was using the bathroom. He moved forward one time too many and a tire hit a hole and the motor home lurched to a stop. The change of momentum catapulted her into the shower a foot away, breaking the shower curtain in the process. The shower curtain was repaired but Andrea's pride was severely damaged.

More than once Ben has had to hit his brakes or a large dip or bump while I was standing or walking in the hallway. The result was that I was ceremoniously catapulted head first down the hall. In those moments I sometimes temporarily lost my battle with my flesh. I really wanted to do something to let him know what he had done to me. It may have not been his fault, but somehow, in that moment, I felt that he could have avoided it. In times like that I found the gift of tongues extremely useful. If you don't speak in tongues, I feel sorry for you.

Orange Juice

When one of your sons spills a whole quart of orange juice in your brand new motor home, it is more than just a little spill. In a regular kitchen, it would be a spill. In a motor home, it's a flood. It gets on the table, the cloth seats, the carpet under the table, the kitchen floor and the cabinets nearby. Liking things clean and new, I hate this kind of a mess. My flesh wants to yell at the boys in anger, asking them why they would do such a thing to me.

By God's grace, I am learning to remember that I am not a victim of someone else's mistakes. Now I can say (gritting my teeth), "I know this was an accident. I know you didn't do this on purpose. I am not going to yell at you. But please be more careful in the future!"

Miracle Motor Home in 2004

Since writing this chapter, while waiting for this book to get published, God miraculously provided the diesel motor home that we had prayed for. After three years and 66,000 miles, the brand new Itasca was no longer brand new. It now had lots of problems, no warranty, and was getting pretty tired. It was obvious that it was designed for vacations, not for a family of four to live in 365 days a year.

A series of miracles allowed us to purchase a 2003 Fleetwood Excursion diesel pusher. It also had been on the lot for a year and had been discounted $45,000. The money for the down payment came in so miraculously that it amazed us.

We now have a larger fridge, more counter space, more comfortable furniture, and more storage space. The décor is also very nice and it's fun to show it off to friends and family and tell them about the miracle God did for us. The diesel engine gets us up and over the mountains in half the time and things have improved a lot. We also have full warrantee protection, which is good, because there have been a number of things that needed to get fixed.

Of course, some things remain the same. Things still fall out when you open cupboard doors. We have a little more space, but we still have to work around each other to get ready for anything. You still can get thrown around if you move around when you are on the road. We still don't have a solid foundation under us, but we are believing that soon we will also find a small place to live while our boys are still with us – perhaps by the time this book is published.

CHAPTER 7

Keeping My Appointments

I don't find this lifestyle very easy although it does have wonderful and eternal rewards. But in spite of the sacrifices and necessity to die to the flesh on a continuous basis, I must go on in the calling of God. My flesh would like to just stay home for a while and be a mother and housewife. Putting a meal together with all the trimmings and having people over in a comfortable home sounds appealing when you have been traveling for five years.

But I know that God has made many very special appointments for me, just like He has for you. We can keep these appointments or we can cancel them. Based on the adventures He has given me in the past few years, I don't want to miss the appointments that are coming in the years ahead. Let me share a few of the experiences that God has given me since we began this journey.

A Small Basement Gathering

Early in our travels, we were invited to do a meeting in a small home. A lady, named Diane, in West Calgary Full Gospel Church, was a real evangelist and had been working with some younger people who had little knowledge of God and lived a pretty rough lifestyle in a poor neighborhood. She led us into a small home and down into a basement, where she played some songs on her guitar. The five or six young people were all interested in God and even enjoyed singing some of the hymns like Amazing Grace, but they really didn't know God. They were a little nervous, being so close to ministers and a couple of them were more or less chain smoking the whole time.

We ministered to each one that night. I spoke to one girl, named Cheryl, telling her in a very emphatic way that God loved her. I shared a few other things that God brought to my mind. She, along with the others, cried and received the words from God. She and most of her friends, including our hosts, immediately began to attend church and are now a faithful part of that fellowship. She has also become a strong evangelist there. Often when we come for meetings there, she invites a number of friends and relatives. We have given words of encouragement to many of them.

Cheryl was baptized in our presence on a later trip to Calgary. What a joy it was to hear her testimony. She told the church that no one had ever looked her in the eye and told her that God loved her before. That one word from the Holy Spirit had made all the difference in her destiny. The next time we came, a young man named Alan, who had met the Lord through her influence, proposed to her publicly in church. The following visit, we were present for their wedding.

We didn't know before we went to that smoke-filled basement in Calgary that a whole group of young adults would begin to walk with God as a result of keeping that appointment. It was just another date on our schedule that God had given us. Now we have some wonderful friends who are walking with God and bringing their children to Sunday School and church. Thank you, Jesus, for that wonderful appointment.

The Jewel-Osco Grocery Clerk

One day in the Chicago area, I was doing some grocery shopping in a Jewel-Osco store. I was standing in line, minding my own business, when the Holy Spirit began to focus me on the clerk. She was busy packing groceries, but I knew God wanted to talk to her. When my turn came, I said, "You're having a hard day, aren't you". She was surprised and nodded in agreement. The Lord gave me more words to share with her and she began to cry while she packed my groceries. "How did you know?" she asked?

"I didn't know, but God does, and He wants you to know that He really loves you." There wasn't a lot of time for follow-up, but she was visibly encouraged and I had to leave her in God's hands, until I had a chance to see her again. She knew that God had chosen to encourage her that day, and she knew that God knew about her situation and that He loved her with all her faults and problems.

Brushing Teeth in an R.V. Park

It happened again in the bathroom of an R.V. park where we happened to be spending the night on our way to our next meetings. Two sinks away from me was a lady brushing her teeth and minding her own business. I really wasn't feeling like intruding on her privacy. But the nudging of the Holy Spirit was very clear, so I stuck my neck out and told her that God wanted her to know about His plan for her and His love which He was asking her to receive.

I don't remember the word, but I sure remember the curious look on her face. I finished the word and left her to think about it. I don't know what she thought about it, but I trust that she was encouraged to know that God cared enough about her to have this grandma interrupt her tooth-brushing activity to give her a word.

Camp Worker Receives God's Love

While spending our second winter at Indian Hills Camp, God arranged another awesome divine appointment. There was a big and tall young man, named Grant, who had an excellent voice, played guitar and wrote music, but he was also a worker at the camp. We had seen him around, but we had no idea that we would be ministering to him at this mostly Baptist camp.

One day I decided to do something to show appreciation to the camp for allowing us to stay on their property with our trailer. Ben did quite a bit of painting for them, but I wanted to do something to help as well. One thing I knew how to do was clean bathrooms, so I found some cleaning materials and set out to clean the ladies' bathrooms that the campers used. It was a long building with many stalls. It would keep me busy for awhile and let the people here know that we wanted to give something back to them.

I had just begun to get into it when Grant entered the doorway with all of his cleaning gear. The first expression on his face said, "What are you doing here?" His voice showed a bit of agitation when he said, "I'm supposed to clean these bathrooms." I prayed a 911 prayer really fast. "Help me, God! What do I do now? This guy isn't happy with me and he's really big!"

Quickly I felt the Spirit of God quiet my spirit and give me a burden for him. I began to tell him that God knew what he was going through, including the depression and the suicidal thoughts. He began to weep and sob and acknowledge that it was all true. From that moment on Ben and I had an open door into his heart. He came out of his depression and began to have hope again that God would use him and his music.

A few weeks later, when we had a meeting in Huntington Beach, California, we invited him to come along and sing for the church. He not only sang his heart-touching testimony songs, but he also played soft music while we ministered to individuals after the preaching. There was definitely a prophetic worship ministry in his life and God used us to reactivate it for the glory of God. We heard from Grant again recently and he has completed and released a CD full of his original songs.

Garage Sale

I have always loved garage sales. So when I drove by a garage sale sign one afternoon in Calgary, Alberta, I decided to check it out. The sale had been well picked over by then, as is normal with garage sales, but God had a special blessing that I had not anticipated.

I was the only customer at the time and God focused me on the mother and daughter that were running the sale. I meandered over to their table and began to engage them in some light conversation. Then the Holy Spirit put some specific words in my mouth and I began to prophesy to them. Of course, I didn't say, "THUS SAITH THE LORD". Nor did I use the word prophecy. I simply said that God wanted them to know that He knew what was going on in their lives and I shared what God was showing me.

Both the mother and daughter were staring at me with a strange look on their face. They asked me how I knew so much about them. Again, I explained the love of God and how I practice listening to His voice so I can encourage other people. They did believe in God, but had very little, if any, relationship with Him. The word from God opened their hearts to the fact that God really did love them and wanted that special relationship with them. I was then able to share my testimony and encourage them to learn to soak with my favorite worship music. I came back later and gave them a couple of my precious worship and soaking CD's.

Sidewalk Appointment

When we are back in Washington State to visit family, we often park our motor home beside Caleb and Barbie's house in Moses Lake. One day we were getting ready to leave Moses Lake and Ben was busy getting the motor home ready for travel. I was busy looking for treats to give my three little brown-eyed grandsons. I had one small bag of chips and I knew I had to find something individual for each of them so they wouldn't fight over one bag. Ben was now ready to go, but I asked him for a few minutes to run to the Shell gas station store about 2 short blocks away.

When he consented, I hurried to the gas station and found two more small bags of chips. On the way home I saw two young gals approaching. The oldest was about 13. Again I felt the Holy Spirit nudging me to speak to them. I took a deep breath and asked God to guide me.

When they got close enough, I said, "Hi girls." Then I told them who I was and that we lived in the motor home a few houses away. I found out that they knew who Barbie was and knew a little about us. With that established, I began to share the word of the Lord. Again, I was careful not to scare them with "Thus saith the Lord", or any reference to prophecy. I simply told them what I believed the Lord wanted them to know. Again, there was a breaking and an opening of the heart to God's love.

When I shared what had happened with Barbie, she informed me that the oldest girl, who was given the word, had been through much pain and abuse. The word God had given me related to her pain and the feeling that she was not loved by God. Again, it was an appointment that God didn't let me break. All I had to do was be obedient and open my mouth and God filled it. Yes, indeed, God is so God!

Las Vegas Bikers

We began ministering in Boulder City and Las Vegas, Nevada in January of 2001. We have returned several times to work with some friends there in a benevolence ministry. They had many friends in Christian biker clubs in the Las Vegas area. They have sponsored a variety of events in the city parks in Boulder City when we were with them. These events were well attended by the Christian bikers in the area.

Most of these bikers had never experienced personal prophetic ministry before and they were kind of in awe that God would show someone else personal things about them to encourage them to serve God with all their hearts. God was really showing them how much He cared about them, even though many of them had been through some terrible experiences before they met God.

After the first bikers were ministered to, they would bring others to our meetings wherever we would be speaking. When these guys would show up on their Harleys, they certainly made a major statement that no one could miss. You could hear their engines blocks away (at least it seemed that way), and they came in with complete biker attire. They had tattoos from here to Ying Yang and black leather everywhere. Some came with wives or girl friends and they were similarly attired.

Some of them looked rather big and mean and they

were certainly not this grandma's comfort zone. My scariest moment came after a big, bald and mean-looking guy that I will call, Sam, sat down in the middle of the room in an aisle seat with his biker wife next to him. He was not giving me any reassuring glances as I began to minister to the full house in a small building in Boulder City. Instead, he was glaring defiantly and almost daring me to mess with him.

I was telling God that I should just let him be and not stir up whatever was occupying his being in front of all those people. But once again, God had a different idea. He kept focusing me on Sam, no matter how much I debated with Him. I argued, "He's big and looks really mean. He doesn't want a woman in his face. Couldn't you have Ben talk to him?" But I failed again to win the argument with God.

I planted myself in front of Sam, not knowing what God wanted me to say. But immediately, God put words in my mouth and very quickly he was fighting back the tears. His wife beside him immediately began sobbing. When we finished with him we ministered to his wife who received her word with gratitude. When we finished with her, Sam stomped out, trying to look tough. He went out the back door into an alley parking area. Our friend reported that when she went outside, she found him on his knees meeting God. He told her that no one knew what "that lady" had told him.

A few days later more bikers showed up on their noisy Harleys. Two more big and tough-looking guys sat at the very back to figure out why their friends had dragged them to this meeting. We ministered to everyone that was there for the first time and eventually we got to the back where these two heavy-weights were waiting their turn. Both of these men had gone through major depression and the Holy Spirit showed me the fact that they were quite suicidal. We prayed the depression and suicide off of them and spoke vision and destiny into their lives. Both of them acknowledged the truth of the word they had received, but one of them especially impacted me.

This tough biker came up to me later and grabbed me by the shoulders and shook me a little. He looked me in the eyes and said, "Lady, you need to hear this. I was going to take my life tonight. I have a loaded gun under my pillow. If God hadn't given you that word for me I would be using that gun tonight."

Can you see why it's so important to keep your appointments? We never know when we will rub shoulders with someone who is at the end of their rope. We never know from the outward appearance what is going on in someone's mind. We are all called to speak for God. See I Peter 4:10,11 and I Corinthians 14. All He wants us to do is listen and then obey. We must keep our appointments if we want the blessings of God in our lives.

CHAPTER 8

Good bye to Comfort Zones

One of the things that God has had me teach people is that God will almost always take you from your comfort zone if you want Him to use you in any significant way. It's too easy just to do the things that we feel good at. It does not make us very dependent on God. Instead we just do what we do without even talking to God about it, much less crying out for His help. God knows that we will never accomplish much and fulfill our destiny if we just do what comes easy. Instead He walks us up to the edge of a cliff and asks us to trust Him enough to take the next step. He asks us to put our feet in the water of the sea or the raging river. Then when we cry out for help, He shows us His amazing and awesome power.

I have been stretched so many times and in so many ways that I feel like a bunch of rubber bands connected to each other. One is stretched in one direction and another in a different direction. But all of them have been extremely stretched at one time or another.

Becoming a Pastor's Wife

After Ben and I were married, I worked the first year while he was in the seminary program of Canadian Theological Seminary at the University of Saskatchewan in Regina. The second year was spent taking a year off to work with Elmer Burnette and Faith Bible Church in Albany, Oregon. Ben was ordained in that ministry and we served in various capacities with youth and children.

After the year was over, we returned to Canada to finish the seminary program. At the same time Ben wanted to stay in ministry, so we took the position of filling the pulpit every Sunday for the Parry Alliance Church in Parry, Saskatchewan, some fifty miles south of Regina. We continued to fill that position for the next four years, adding another night to work with the youth of the church.

After Ben's graduation with his Master of Divinity degree, the people of the church in Parry were willing to have us move there and be their first full-time pastors. This was a big step for them and they were trusting God for enough finances to give us the mini-salary that would just barely meet our needs. We loved the people and were willing to go there and see what God would do through us.

That's when some very interesting stretching began to occur. The church made arrangements with a local farmer, who owned a vacant old farmhouse a few miles from town.

The Bathroom

I'll never forget when they showed me my new bathroom. They took me down into a dirt-floored cellar and showed me a five gallon bucket with a toilet seat on top. The cellar was also the home of many mice and even some gardener snakes. This was not what this Seattle girl was accustomed to, and I wasn't too excited about the prospect.

It wasn't long until I prevailed on my husband to get me a chemical porta-potty so I wouldn't have to go down into that basement any more. Ben still had to empty the potty every other day or so, but we could have it upstairs and it didn't smell too bad. We had running water in the small kitchen sink, but that was rather brown because it was pumped from a dugout a little ways from the house.

Taking a bath would be a different story. There was no bath tub and no bathroom. There was an old bath tub out in the yard, however. It had been used for a pig trough for who knows how long. Some of the folk helped us clean it up and haul it into the house. We put it in the closed-in porch at the unused entrance to the house.

Taking a bath required heating and hauling many buckets of water from the kitchen to the porch, which was from one end of the house to the other. Ben, who was raised to handle any kind of lifestyle took it in stride and willingly filled my bathtub with the light brown water, which we had heated on the propane stove.

Surprise in the Toaster

After returning from a short trip to Regina, I decided to make toast for my little Kenny, who was nearly one year old at the time. I put a piece of bread in one side of the toaster and pushed it down. Then I heard a strange noise in the toaster. I picked it up to look at it and all of a sudden chaos erupted in my kitchen as a surprised little mouse came flying out of the toaster, practically in my face. Who knows, I may have toasted his tail a little bit, and I'm sure that little mouse was also finding himself well out of his own comfort zone.

In case you haven't guessed, I don't like snakes, spiders or mice, and this mouse totally freaked me out. I threw the toaster in the air and ran out of the room screaming for Ben, while poor little Kenny was still in his high chair wondering what was chasing his not-so-brave mother. This experience added another phobia to the hundreds already on the list. It is "toaster-phobia". I never used the toaster after that without first nervously checking it for unwanted guests.

Country Telephones

Another stretching experience came when we received a call from our college friends, who phoned to tell us they were coming for a visit. A few minutes later there was a knock on our door. One of our church members was at our door with a nice bag of meat and vegetables. She announced that she had heard that we were having company and wanted to help us feed them.

When we asked how she had heard about it, she just laughed. "Oh, you know, out here, if you get a call, half the town listens in." Each family had a particular ring on the good old party line, but there was not much happening in Parry, so everyone wanted to know what was happening with their neighbors. After that, we were a little more careful about what we said over the phone, especially about our church members. Actually, we dearly loved all our members. They were simple farmers but they had totally won our hearts.

Leaving Parry

If God hadn't intervened, we may have stayed in Parry a long time, but God had other plans for us. In addition to having little Kenny, who is now a pastor, in spite of what I put him through, I was also very pregnant with Barbie. By the way, we didn't realize what we had done, naming our first two kids, Ken and Barbie. They were named after family members. It wasn't until Ken and Barbie went to college together, when Ken had changed his name from "Kenny" to "Ken" that they began to get teased for being Ken and Barbie dolls.

That year we had one of the worst winters we had ever experienced in Saskatchewan. Snow storms had come from every direction and with strong winds they formed a circle of drifts around our house. The drifts got higher and higher until we had to climb a shear wall of snow to get out of our yard. For a few feet around the house there was virtually no snow but suddenly you would run into a wall of snow. The snow plows would not even plow our road, because there were no school children on our road and they only plowed for the school buses in those days.

In the prairies of Canada, everyone has what they called "block heaters" to keep the motor oil from getting too cold to start the car in below zero weather. Everyone plugged their car in at night to keep the engine warm. Our problem was that we had to keep getting longer extension cords to plug in our car, because we had to park farther and farther away.

Another interesting result of the snow was that the pigs, that were being raising on the farm where our house was, would walk right over the tall fence meant to keep them away from the house. The drifts were so high that the fences were totally buried in the snow. The pigs just walked right on over and watched us eat our breakfast, looking right into the windows.

Because of the snow and accessibility problems, our church elders were getting very concerned that I wouldn't be able to get out quick if I went into labor. I was due in February, according to our doctor and the snow would not melt much until March or April. They didn't want us to resign the church, but they thought we should move into Regina for awhile.

Because we thought that Barbie would be born soon, we moved into the basement of one of Ben's aunts who lived in Regina and worked at the Bible College and Seminary, where Ben and I had attended. It was a very trying experience for me, knowing that everyone was waiting for me to have my baby so we could go on with our life.

The move out of Parry was not an easy thing either. I was very pregnant and we couldn't get a car or truck anywhere near the house. Ben and my mom, who came from Seattle to help us out, started with just a toboggan until someone came to the rescue and loaned us their snowmobile.

My mom and Ben made many snowmobile trips from the car to the house and back to the car, hauling load after load on a toboggan behind the snowmobile. Then they would bring one carload back to Regina.

Hospital Politics

I loved surgery and enjoyed working with the people on our surgery team, although there were times when being at the bottom of the totem pole was not the most fun place to be. There were times when I had to take the blame for things that were not at all my fault, but it was another way that God was teaching me that this life was not going to be fair all the time and I would just have to deal with it.

Several times people above me took advantage of me to give themselves more benefits and demoted me in ways that were not to anyone's advantage except theirs. Once or twice I tried to stand up for my rights, but the emotional price I paid was quite high and I was not so sure it had been worth it.

Near the end of my time in the small hospital, which I had served for about 12 years, there were some very hot and emotional debates taking place in the hospital, regarding whether or not to keep the present hospital administrator, and everyone seemed to be taking sides. Our vascular surgeon was very determined to have things go his way and others on the team were secretly on the other side. I was not committed to either side and wanted everyone to get along in peace and harmony.

Being involved in hostile political debates is certainly not my comfort zone. But everyone expected me to be on their side and tried to convince me that they were right. Things got very explosive when the surgeon discovered that some of his team were not with him and were actually campaigning for the other side, and he also thought that I was on the other side of the debate. The surgical suite was about as icy as you could imagine. Surgery was no longer fun.

Things never really got back to normal. God was actually preparing me to let go of my natural security. We had been pastoring a small church and Christian school, which we had run without tuition, as a way to reach out to a needy community. The regular income had been such a help and blessing to us and I had enjoyed feeling fulfilled in the hospital. I had many opportunities to pray with people as they were being wheeled into the surgical suite. I had total freedom to pray out loud for them if they asked me to, and it was a great way to touch people's lives. So many times I saw God bring peace to them as I prayed.

Moving to Spokane

But God was planning to move us on to new things and He knew I needed to be able to let go. The day finally came when Ben announced to the family that God had clearly spoken to us that our days in Willapa Harbor were coming quickly to an end. We would be transitioning the Paul Turner family into the leadership of the church and I would have to quit my job at the hospital. I had many mixed emotions, but I was emotionally drained from the stress at the hospital and I was finally ready to release my job to the Lord, and trust God for the future.

But this was not going to be easy. In the days to follow I would discover how great a woman of faith that I wasn't. I wanted very much to trust God for our finances and future, but every step of the way, I had to fight the anxiety and fear of not having the provision we needed for basic necessities.

We felt called to move to Spokane and thought that we might be launched from there to missionary evangelism work in the Yucatan in Mexico. That didn't pan out, but God had other plans to retrain us and redirect our paths. We became a part of a prophetic church and convention center for the first year. During that year we had many opportunities to train and develop our prophetic gifts. That's when I discovered that God was putting a strong anointing on my life to prophesy encouragement to people.

Practicing the Prophetic Gift

For example, a big conference with several hundred people was held at our church. There were four well-known prophetic speakers ministering to the people. A few folk had received words from them, but most were just soaking in the public ministry. I had been volunteered to serve in the nursery, a job which I was very accustomed to after being a pastor's wife for so many years.

The job was complicated by the fact that there was a youth conference going on next door to where I was trying to take care of too many kids with Veggie Tales and whatever else was available. The youth leaders believed in radical and very loud music, which easily permeated the thin walls of our nursery room. After several hours, I had a massive headache and finally got to take a quick break.

I headed into the sanctuary to see what was happening. Immediately, the Lord focused me on a lady sitting at the back. He impressed on my spirit to go over and give her a word. I did what I often do. Like Moses, I argued with God. I told God that this lady wanted a word from one of those "Big Prophets" at the front. Somehow, I thought that God would appreciate this information, but for some reason, He didn't seem to be impressed with my response to His prompting. Instead, He spoke to me, "If you don't give her a word, she will go home without one."

I received the rebuke and walked over to the lady. I asked her if I could minister to her. She said, "Oh, yes!" So I began to speak what God was putting on my heart and the words just poured out like Niagara Falls. She began to sob and explode with emotion. Her mascara was running down her face. Her nose was running even worse and she was bent over on the floor convulsing with emotion. She was a total mess! The words just kept pouring for several minutes, and although we didn't have a tape recorder to record the prophetic encouragement, I believe she will never be the same. When I was done, she just said, "Thank you, Oh thank you!" I said, "Thank Jesus." and went back to the nursery.

It was not my comfort zone to prophesy in the presence of the well-known prophets. I was worried that other people might have thought that I was trying to impress someone and get attention like I've seen others do. But I knew I had to obey God. That's what it's all about. Obey God and let Him take you out of your comfort zone, or you won't fulfill your destiny and find the fulfillment that only obedience can bring.

Trusting God for Finances

The problem was we didn't have a whole lot of income. Ben took the first job he could find, when we moved to Spokane, delivering pizza for Pizza Hut. It was a job that didn't require a long-term commitment, and Ben felt that we should be free to go on ministry teams and take trips to various places where God was calling us. It was a bit humbling for both of us and not exactly what you'd expect from someone with a master's degree, but the nightly tips helped us with groceries and daily needs.

I had a few months of unemployment insurance, which was a blessing. When that ended, Ben starting working for an evangelist, while still delivering Pizza at night. He did his bookings, and also helped write his newsletters and designed the brochures for a major conference. That job lasted for a few months and was a big blessing.

After one year the ministry we had come to train under began to fold up. We had already taken a trip or two on our own and one or two with the ministry we had trained under. God had been blessing these trips and people seemed hungry for the ministry that we brought to them. It encouraged us that we were on the right track.

The second year in Spokane we helped our son and daughter-in-law, Ken and Valencia, start a new church and Christian School in the Spokane Valley. We also took a few more trips to Chicago and Calgary. Income came in little bits and pieces and we did without many things and struggled to pay bills on time. It was a real time of testing and I so wanted to get a full-time job to take the pressure off.

But Ben was sure that I was not to be tied down, and there were no openings for O.R. Techs anyway. Besides that I had lost my training certificate in all the moving, so I couldn't prove that I had the academic qualifications, even though I had over fifteen years of experience. Trying to get records from the teaching hospital in Regina, where I had trained, also proved fruitless.

My last resort was to go back to waitressing. I had waitressed in several great restaurants before I became a surgical tech. So I applied for a job at a local Marie Calender's restaurant and was accepted. I thought this would be easy. I had always done well at this trade since I loved to serve, and God had always given me favor with people I worked for. I thought the schedule might be flexible enough to accommodate our occasional trips out of town.

This job however, brought a whole lot of pain and trouble. Although there were days when I was blessed with favor with my customers, it seemed like there was no way to please my supervisors and it almost took an act of congress to get a day off for a weekend ministry trip. Finally, Ben asked me to quit the job and trust God. Mercifully, God made it quite clear, with a very stressful experience at work, that He didn't really want me there in the first place, and He didn't need my help to bring in the finances. My mom had always worked, so I always tended to feel responsible to jump in and do my share to help with the finances.

Slowly, but surely, our ministry invitations were increasing. I did my first speaking at Aglow meetings and a ladies retreat. God greatly blessed these meetings and confirmed the call He had on my life to speak and prophesy encouragement to His people. Ben had real faith in my calling and destiny, even when I doubted, and he encouraged me that God was going to use me greatly. The offerings taken in those days were not very large, but they helped us a lot and always encouraged us that God could take care of us.

Finally, folks in Chicago gave us a thirty-three foot trailer and we knew we were to hit the road full-time. That story of transition trauma is recorded in the first chapter of this book, but what I want to reaffirm is that this financial limb that we stepped out on was even more scary than trying to live off of a Pizza Hut income. We had no health insurance, no salary of any kind, and we still had plenty of old bills to pay off. In fact, there were still old medical and dental bills along with a few other debts from past emergencies.

The amazing thing was that even though we went through some very slow times as far as our ministry schedule was concerned, the old bills began to get paid off, little by little. The transition trauma was basically over for the time being. We had begun to embrace the purpose of God for our life and our destiny calling. We had fewer problems paying our bills during this time than during the days when we were both working as well as in those two years of transition. God was confirming that we were in the center of His will and purpose for our lives.

Since those early days we have seen God do so many financial miracles. We have never let people know when we were under financial stress, but God has always made a way where there seemed to be no way. We have had plenty of tests and trials and often wish that God would come through before the pressure got so great, but so many times it seemed that He was waiting for us to get on our faces and cry out to him. When we do that, we usually see a major breakthrough very quickly.

Launched into Prophetic Ministry

The biggest loss of comfort zone, was when I knew God was calling me to travel around the country and the world giving prophetic words to people I didn't know. All my life I've had a problem opening my big mouth at the wrong time. My mouth had gotten me into so much trouble as a pastor's wife that my husband had to be the janitor cleaning up the messes I left behind.

Becoming a full-time prophetic person was scary. In the first place, I know that a lot of people have hated prophets. They killed them! There are Jezebels out there who want to destroy them. This was definitely not my comfort zone. I like people to like me. It has always bothered me if someone said or implied something negative about me. I felt like God was hanging me on the edge of a cliff and someone was going to step on my fingers.

I never asked God for this ministry, and like Moses, I have argued quite often with His choice. But somehow, I lost every argument and God said, "Go, speak to my people that I have come to deliver them from their bondages." Since then, we have seen many troubled people delivered from suicide and from so many other forms of satanic oppression.

Yes, we have encountered some severe attacks. Like someone said, "The anointing brings the attack." Some of our attacks have come from people we trusted and loved. We were quite naïve to the fact that Christians could be so mean and tell flat-out lies because they couldn't control you. Slander and gossip have at times been quite vicious.

But the good news is that God always turns the evil intentions of the enemy into good. The plans of satan have failed and God has continued to bless us. For every person who has attacked us, there are probably a thousand who have shown us love and gratefulness for touching their lives. If I can keep this in perspective, it helps me go on to touch another needy life.

A Most Unusual Security Guard

Recently, Ben suggested that I fly from Chicago to Calgary a few days before the big ladies' retreat at Circle Square Ranch. The advantage would be that I wouldn't have to endure the long motor home ride for three of four days and I would have that time to be alone with God. A friend in Calgary managed a tower apartment building and had a guest apartment which we have used several times.

My hesitation was three-fold. First of all, I didn't want to be separated from my family. I want to be with them if anything negative should happen on the road. I know I should trust God more than I do, but as a mother and wife, I want to be with my family. Secondly, I didn't really want to spend the extra money, when I knew we still had bills to pay. For this hesitation, I asked God for a sign. If He would miraculously provide the money for the ticket, I would know He wanted me to fly. The answer came a couple of days later when a young couple told Ben they wanted to buy my plane ticket to Calgary, not knowing I had set this out as a fleece.

My third reason for hesitating was that I was nervous about something regarding the location of that apartment. The apartment was on the fifth floor of the tower. That floor also had a roof-top jogging track that ran right beside the window to my apartment. The window did not lock well, and I had seen some strange-looking characters on that roof. The other times I had been there, Ben had been with me, but now I would be alone. But since God had provided my ticket, I knew that God would take care of me.

When I was brought to my apartment in Calgary, I was told that something unusual had happened on the roof. A pair of Canada Geese had chosen a flower pot, just outside my window, to lay their eggs. Being protected by the government, no one could move their nest or bother them.

Actually, no one dared to bother them. The male goose stood guard at the entrance to the roof track. One brave maintenance man had tried to do some work on the roof and the "guard goose" had attacked him and injured him.

When I opened the window drapes to look outside, the mother goose hissed at me ferociously.

I decided that God had directed that pair of geese to lay their eggs by my window to show how much He loved me and understood the weakness of my faith. I was able to spend the next two or three days soaking and seeking God for guidance, without having to be nervous about who was out on the track outside my window. My "guard geese" were like God's guardian angels, sent to bring peace to my heart and soul.

CHAPTER 9

Warring with the Prophetic

Paul told Timothy to wage a good warfare using the prophetic words that he had been given. We have had many words from other men and women of God that have encouraged us over the years and helped us not to quit when things got tough. Years ago we had a powerful experience when three prophets from Portland City Church, then known as Portland Bible Temple, spoke over us in what was called a "Presbytery Service".

These men began by speaking some powerful things over Ben. Then they turned to me and began to speak to me about coming out of the shadows and ministering beside my husband. They said that I too would be ministering to women and children and that I would be an effective communicating servant of God, working as a partner with Ben. That took a long time to be fulfilled, but now that is exactly what has been happening. I had also been told that I have the gift of faith and prophecy, but it didn't seem like it at the time.

But because of these words and others, which were re-corded and transcribed, I kept believing that it would be a part of my destiny. When I felt defeated, I was reminded of God's promise to me and kept going with His strength. The greatest object lesson of the power of the prophetic came with an experience we had with our second daughter, Andrea. This experience will always be a source of encouraging others to wage a good warfare with their prophetic words.

To the Brink of Death and Back

Andrea had struggled with asthma for years. Our home in the woods on the very wet coast of Washington was filled with mildew which stirred up her allergies. One night at about three or four in the morning, she woke me up with a severe attack. I quickly took her into the hospital where I worked. The nurse on duty felt she just needed a nebulizer treatment, which she administered and sent us home. I thought the doctor should see her, but I didn't want to act like I didn't trust her.

We returned home and had just gotten into the house when Andrea turned to me and said, "Mom, take me back!" I turned to look at her and saw the oxygen leaving her body. She was losing all the color in her skin. I began to cry out to God and call for Ben to come and help me. Ben came and called the ambulance. Then we got Andrea into the Taurus. Ben, still in his robe, began to drive toward town to meet the ambulance.

As soon as we got her into the car, Andrea seized up with her mouth closed. I knew I had to give her artificial resuscitation, so I pried her mouth open and began to breath hard into her lungs. I didn't know her lungs had collapsed and that she needed more than the normal level of resuscitation, but somehow God impressed upon me to breath hard.

While Ben was driving as fast as possible around the coastal highway curves, he was taking Andrea's pulse. At least he was trying to. Sometimes he found it, but would lose it very quickly. Before we reached the ambulance, coming from Raymond, at the bottom of the hospital hill in South Bend, Washington, Andrea had a cardiac arrest. But during the whole time driving the twelve to fifteen miles, I was warring with the prophetic.

Andrea had recently received a strong prophetic word from Doug Sherman, a young prophet from Moses Lake, Washington. He had seen her doing drama, mime and worship and attending some kind of a Bible School. He had spoken other things, such as evangelism and working with youth and turning them towards God. She was still a junior in high school and had not yet fulfilled her calling.

I began to do warfare with the words I knew were from God. I said, "God, You said that Andrea would do drama and mime and other things in your Kingdom. You've got to bring her back to us. I refuse to let her go without her fulfilling her destiny." After reminding God of His promise, I would breath hard into her lungs again, praying silently as I breathed. Again, I reminded God of Andrea's destiny, and would not quit claiming the fulfillment of His words.

By the time we arrived at the hospital behind the ambulance, my surgical team had arrived. The surgeon took charge and everyone began to work on her. Then the surgeon turned to Ben and me, and asked us to leave the room. I knew what that meant. They were going to have to take serious measures and didn't want us watching. My heart kept crying out to God and claiming Andrea's destiny.

I took one last look at her lifeless body before I left the room. Suddenly, I saw her fingers move. Nothing really had been done to her yet and I knew that God had brought her back. She recovered quickly and was back with us in no time. She shared that while she was gone from us she had felt a powerful peace and knew she was in the presence of the Lord. She had always been afraid to die, thinking that she might have done something to offend the Lord. After this experience, she lost her fear of death and is the "gutsiest" little thing you could imagine. She has lived in ghetto neighborhoods in Dallas and is not afraid to go wherever she feels like to witness or whatever.

Andrea has fulfilled almost every word that God gave her in her teens. She has majored in drama and has done drama and mime in many places, both in America and overseas, including Poland and the Ukraine. She taught drama for a Bible School in Poland one summer, and she has also taught drama at a Christian High School and impacted many teens for Christ.

How to Become a Math Whiz

One evening we ministered to some families in Calgary, Alberta, at a home meeting. I told one of the teenage boys that God had given him a good mind for math and science.

I didn't know it but this young man was having a terrible struggle with math. Years before he had been told by one of his teachers that he couldn't learn math. Now he was preparing to take a series of final exams as a high school senior.

He had been failing almost every test up until this point, and was extremely discouraged and down on himself. Shortly after this word, he took his first test and failed it just like he normally did. His mother had an unusual faith and tenacity. She took this word through me as a word from God and began to do warfare with her son. She reminded him of what I had spoken to him and said, "We are going to believe what God said. God said you are good at math and you are going to get good scores on your exams." His next test showed a little improvement and they continued to do warfare and claimed the prophetic word for him.

He did even better on the next one, scoring in the 70's and was gaining confidence with each exam. Finally, he told his mom, "I think I can get a 90% on the next test." He took the test and scored 100%. His whole family was overjoyed.

They had learned the true power of warring with their prophetic word. The word had the power to break off the lies of the deceiver, and warring for the fulfillment released the gifting that had been buried for many years.

CHAPTER 10

Teaching Teamwork

One of the most exciting things that God is bringing us into is teamwork. We are always exhorting people to activate their gifts, but often they don't have a lot of help in learning how to use their gifts. When they can work with others as part of a team, it gives them a wonderful chance to practice their gifts under the supervision of more mature leaders. Having teams allows us to divide the responsibilities and enables us to minister to more people. But functioning in teamwork can be a challenge and requires a commitment to pay the price that is required.

The Price of Teamwork

Working together with almost anyone, including your husband or wife takes patience and determination. Many people have commented on how united Ben and I are and how our marriage is such a beautiful example to others. I don't want to burst anyone's bubble, but we have had plenty of rough times, and still occasionally do, when our unity is not exactly totally wonderful. We try not to embarrass each other publicly, but we have to deal with our differences just like everyone else.

What God has been asking us to do is to be honest with people and let them know that we are flesh like they are, but because we are committed to edifying the body of Christ and growing the Kingdom of God, we learn to deal with our differences and fight for the unity that God has given us by His Holy Spirit. Frankly, in the past, even though we have been married for over thirty-five years, we hardly ever ministered together side-by-side. Ben did the preaching and administration of the church and school. I worked in the nursery, Children's Church, the Learning to Read class, the girls' clubs, as well as the hospital, and I did a lot of the counseling with the women who had numerous problems in the church.

We have now been working together, ministering side-by-side for several years at this writing. We have learned a lot, but we still have to learn to be patient with each other and take our turn when it comes. I have heard many of Ben's favorite messages dozens of times, and he has heard my stories just as often. When we minister prophetically, I am more high intensity and usually take the lead. Ben waits while I share and then I wait while he shares. Often we both have something at the same time, but one of us has to yield to the other. We have learned to do this, but it doesn't necessarily come naturally. It takes work! We have learned to use our waiting time to pray and to prepare for our next turn so we are ready to release a more impacting word from God.

Our personalities are also very different. I am spontaneous and impulsive, while Ben is more of a thinker and conservative in many ways. He loves sports and doesn't care for shopping. I often get irritated with sports, but I love to shop for special things for kids, grandkids and people I minister to at retreats, etc. Ben is also a person who likes to get the facts and numbers as accurate as possible, while I try to get across the emotional impact of the event in as exciting a way as possible.

The Benefits

The Bible reveals many benefits of working as a team. It says that "One will chase a thousand, two will chase ten thousand." (Deuteronomy 32:30). Jesus also promised that if any two agree in prayer for anything they asked, it would be done by His Father in Heaven. (Matthew 18:19). We are also told in Ecclesiastes that there is an advantage to working together. For example, when one falls, the other one can pick him up. Please read the following four verses.

Two are better than one, because they have a good reward for their labor. For if they fall, one will lift up his companion. But woe to him who is alone when he falls, for he has no one to help him up. Again, if two lie down together, they will keep warm; But how can one be warm alone? Though one may be overpowered by another, two can withstand him.

And a threefold cord is not quickly broken.
(Ecclesiastes 4:9-12)

We know that the reason the devil fights unity in our relationship, as he does with all Christians, is because he fears the damage that we will do to his kingdom if we unite our hearts and our gifts for the sake of the Kingdom of God. We have had numerous prophetic words telling us that God has ordained for us to work in unity, and that we are far more effective working together than we would be working separately. That doesn't mean that we can't minister without our mate, but because we have developed the unity by working with each other, we carry the anointing of that unity, even when we do occasionally minister without each other.

Without Ben's encouragement, I doubt that I would have much of a ministry today. There have been so many times that I felt like quitting. And Ben maintains that it makes a big difference to his preaching, having me breaking the ice with my stories before he takes the mike. While I share my stories, he is fine tuning his thoughts and getting more clarity on what God wants him to share. We have developed an interdependence that makes us ten times as strong.

One great advantage of teamwork is that together we have more gifts in operation, which can at times make a critical difference. For instance, one of us may be taken in with someone who is very gifted and charismatic in personality.

The other one, however, may discern a problem and caution the first one to go slowly and be careful making hasty decisions or commitments. We have been protected numerous times because we have learned to listen to each other.

Another example is that one of us may discern by a word of knowledge that a person has a need for physical healing. The other one may have an anointing of faith for healing to pray for the miracle. God does delight in dividing up His gifts to give us all specialty functions in the body of Christ, and then bringing the gifts all together to accomplish His purpose, just like the different parts of our own physical bodies work together to accomplish what we do.

Adding Team Members

Early in our traveling ministry, we brought along a gifted soloist, named Carol, whose music was powerfully anointed. I first brought her along to a ladies' retreat in Calgary, and then later we took her to Chicago for some meetings there.

This new dimension to our teamwork required more adjustments to the way we ministered. For one thing doing the ministry with three people, instead of two, meant a further sharing of the ministry time. The soloist was very gracious and very willing to communicate and work with us, but once again, we had to work at making it work.

The blessing and anointing, however, were much increased as we worked together. The result and impact of adding Carol's anointing to ours was dramatic, and well worth the small adjustments we had to make.

As The Deer

I shared earlier the story about the deer jumping up and down at the ladies retreat at Enthios, near Calgary in the fall of 2001. We began to jump just like the deer and God blessed us with an awesome breakthrough and an explosion of His presence and powerful ministry from lady to lady.

That was the retreat where three ladies from Chicago and two from Washington State had come to help me minister. The powerful part of that whole event was that all five ladies found themselves used by God in wonderful ways that had never happened before. In addition, so many more people received ministry than would have without them. It was a real revelation of the power of teamwork to multiply the anointing to multiply the ministry potential.

Gathering the Troops in Nevada

In January, 2003, we headed to Nevada for our third visit to the Las Vegas and Boulder City region. Again, we invited others to join us for a long weekend of activities, which would include outreach in the Boulder City park and the streets of Las Vegas. A total of thirty-seven people responded, including a worship leader from Idaho, a dozen folk from Alberta, a dozen from Illinois, and a dozen from Dallas. The latter group included our daughter, Andrea, who helped lead a Christ For the Nations Institute drama and dance team. Many of them had ministered in similar situations in other nations, as well as in the U.S.

With so many people from so many different places, the dynamics of teamwork had to change radically again. There were a few challenges to deal with, but the impact was awesome, both in the community, and on the visiting ministry team. Many people, especially from Canada and Illinois, took their own personal gifts and ministries to a much higher level. Most of them have gone on to use their prophetic gifts in new ways since that trip to Nevada. The result is that many folk have been blessed and encouraged through their gifts.

More Teamwork at Circle Square Ranch

In May, 2003, there was a regional ladies retreat held northeast of Calgary at the Circle Square Ranch, where I was invited to be the speaker. I issued an invitation to a number of ladies whom I thought might be able to join me as part of a team.

The most awesome thing about teamwork is that it takes people's eyes off of the one person who is supposed to be some kind of a superstar. Instead, there is a team of no-name people who work together to try to hear from God and minister to a person who is crying out for a word from God. Then only God gets the glory and not one person.

Anyway, about fifteen ladies decided to join us for the retreat called, "A Hallelujah Hoedown." There were about one hundred and fifty ladies registered, more than ever before and so having a team made a huge difference. Again, some of these ladies were getting their first dose of this kind of ministry. They had never been part of a team that would stand together for up to three or four hours, focusing to listen for God's voice and then share it when their time came. For some if was quite an emotional energy drain, but all of them enjoyed developing their gifts and serving on a team.

One of our good friends from Chicago not only ministered but received powerful ministry from other members of the team. She has reported that her life has never been the same and that she was set free from things that she had been fighting all her life. That wasn't because of the speaker, it was because we had a team that could hear from God and because the many gifts of the Holy Spirit were working together through the different team members.

Ben and I have been getting many calls and confirming words concerning several African nations as well as Great Britain and India. We expect to be making more overseas trips in the near future. Our strong desire is to take as many people along as possible. We know that we will all see the powerful hand of God at work in many of these nations, where signs and wonders are much more common.

We know that once people have tasted of the supernatural power of God, they will never be normal again. Rather, they will be bringing a contagious passion and hunger for more of God's anointing for their own nation and churches. They will all be saying, "God is so God!" Everyone will win except the devil, and we don't feel a bit sorry for him.

FINAL CONCLUSION

God Is So God!

Let's face it. None of us are perfect or deserve to be used by Him! But God is just so God! He knows the weaknesses of all of his servants, including the most famous ministry "superstars". But He chooses to use all of us who decide to dedicate their lives to serve Him. I often wonder why He chose me, knowing how many problems I had. I see others that God is using in much greater ways, and I notice that they aren't perfect either.

God has led us in unusual ways, but in all our circumstances He has proven that He is God and we are not. If I were God I would surely have given up on me, but I'm not God and He has proven to me that He most certainly is.

I never asked God for a position or title, and I never dreamed of traveling around and speaking and prophesying to thousands of people every year. I didn't feel worthy and I would be happy just to be a wife and mother and have my kids and grandkids over for Thanksgiving dinners and other special events. I'm not jealous of other woman speakers or men speakers for that matter. I'm just a simple Seattle girl who sang that simple song, "Yes Lord, Yes Lord, Yes, Yes Lord!" And God took me at my word and chose me to be an example for other simple gals from anywhere who also will sing that simple song.

If you are willing to fall down a thousand times and keep getting up, and if you are willing to be a servant instead of a superstar, if you sing that simple song and mean it, then God will use you too. And He will use you far more than you could ever expect or imagine. All you need is to be willing to die. Yes, He's going to kill you, and that's a good thing! It's a good thing because when you die, He lives in you. And when He lives in you, He does incredible things through you.

Ending with the Beginning

I want to end this book with the story of how my life began. I learned about the events of my birth just a few years ago. My father was a Navy man, just home from World War II, and I was a baby-boomer baby. But when my mother was going through the delivery, the doctor informed my dad that I was trapped in the birth canal and he thought he was going to lose us both, the way my mom was hemorrhaging.

My dad was not a religious person, but he knew there was a God and he ran out of the hospital and into the first church he could find. He ran up to the front and threw himself down at the altar. He told God that if He would spare both our lives, he would give this baby to Him. Very quickly, after this prayer, God pushed my little body right out of the birth canal and both my mother and I escaped the fate the doctor had predicted.

For some reason and through a series of events, I chose to attend a Christian high school called Kings Gardens in Seattle. Besides babysitting, I worked at the Kings Garden Nursing Home part time to pay my way through. And through another series of events which included an uncle leaving me a small inheritance, and having a boy friend whose brother had been to Bible College, I decided to go to the same Bible College, which happened to be Canadian Bible College in Regina.

As I boarded the train to head for Regina, my dad, who had really wanted me to go into the medical field, stood at the station with tears streaming down his face. I know he didn't want to let me go, but I believe that He remembered the promise He had made to God over eighteen years before. There was no natural reason that I should want to go to Bible school, but God had heard my dad's desperate cry for mercy. He also remembered my dad's promise to surrender me to the Lord and God took him at his word.

At Bible College God quickly revealed to me that He wanted me to break up with the young man that I had come with. Right after breaking up, I was with my room-mate setting tables in the dining room. I was telling her that I had gotten the grades required for dating, while the boy-friend I came with had not. I didn't see the young man in a royal blue sports jacket standing on the stairs listening to what I was saying. Thinking I was still committed to my former boyfriend, he teased me saying, "I think I'll take you up on that." Something inside of me said, "Yes."

Soon Ben and I were spending time together whenever it was allowed, and he began to share from his heart his passion for revival, prayer and the Holy Spirit and His gifts. He believed that God still could heal and do all the miracles recorded in the Bible. He was spending time alone with God every morning in intercession for the church to have revival. I had never been taught many of the things he was teaching me, but somehow I knew it was true.

My days at Bible College were exciting times for me. They were times of great social activities, practical and not-so-practical jokes, and lots of fun and laughter. I got involved with my missionary kid friend, Marilyn Irwin, in several pranks which often landed us in trouble with the Dean of Women. Fortunately, neither of us were kicked out for our indiscretions. I did have lots of fun and enjoyed the social life, but the best part of the whole Bible college experience was the deep spiritual growth happening in my life and the sense of destiny that God was giving me.

Although it was not a totally smooth journey from our first encounter to the wedding ceremony, we were married on August 11, 1967. From that date on, we have found God to be there in all the affairs of our life, even when we hurt Him and failed to function in His grace and love. But He would always come to restore us when we were willing to face our need and reach out to Him.

All I can say as I look back and see the workmanship of God woven into the fabric of our lives is,

"GOD IS SO GOD!"

AUTHOR PROFILE

Brenda Peters

Brenda Peters is the mother of five God-serving children, and wife of Ben Peters. She has served in ministry for over thirty-five years in a multitude of capacities including children and women's ministries as a pastor's wife, teaching phonetics in their Christian school, and serving as an operating room technician in both large and small hospitals.

Brenda's reputation as a ladies' speaker has growing rapidly since the couple left their church in Raymond, Washington, in 1997, after fifteen years of service there. She has now ministered in numerous ladies meetings, large ladies retreats and conferences, both in North America and overseas. Brenda's style of ministry is very practical, dynamic, entertaining and heart-impacting. Under the name, Open Heart Ministries, both Ben and Brenda focus on touching people's hearts, to open them up to God's love, and to encourage them to serve God with all their hearts.

Brenda grew up in Seattle and then attended Canadian Bible College, in Regina, Saskatchewan, where she met her husband, Ben. They have served together as pastors of a small country church, as associate pastors to a man with a strong healing and deliverance anointing, and also as pastors of Willapa Harbor Christian Fellowship and Christian Fellowship Academy, which they founded in 1983, in Raymond, Washington.

When not doing ladies meetings, Brenda usually co-ministers with Ben and flows not only with a strong speaking ministry, but also with a strong prophetic anointing.

Open Heart Ministries

With over 35 years of ministry experience, Ben Peters with his wife, Brenda, have been called to an international apostolic ministry of equipping and activating others. As founders and directors of Open Heart Ministries, Ben and Brenda have ministered to tens of thousands with teaching and prophetic ministry. The result is that many have been saved, healed and delivered and activated into powerful ministries of their own.

Ben has been given significant insights for the body of Christ and has written eight books in the past five years, since beginning a full-time itinerant ministry. His passions and insights include unity in the body of Christ, accessing the glory of God, five-fold team ministry and signs and wonders for the world-wide harvest.

The Peters not only minister at churches, camps, retreats and conferences, but also host numerous conferences with cutting-edge apostolic and prophetic leaders. They reside now in Northern Illinois with the youngest three of their five children, and travel extensively internationally.

Open Heart Ministries
www.ohmint.org
benrpeters@juno.com
15648 Bombay Blvd.
S. Beloit, IL 61080

LaVergne, TN USA
24 May 2010
183738LV00002B/9/A